Darina Allen

SIMPLY
DELICIOUS FISH

Gill and Macmillan
and
Radio Telefís Éireann

Published by
Gill and Macmillan Ltd
Goldenbridge
Dublin 8
and
Radio Telefís Éireann
Donnybrook
Dublin 4
© Darina Allen 1991
0 7171 1822 3
Photographs by Des Gaffney, RTE
Food styling by Rory O'Connell
Design by Peter Larrigan
Typeset by Irish Typesetters, Galway
Colour origination by Irish Photo Ltd, Dublin
Printed by Butler & Tanner, Somerset

To the memory of Tommy Sliney,
who gave away more fish than he ever sold.

By the same author:
Simply Delicious
Simply Delicious 2
A Simply Delicious Christmas

Contents

The items marked with an asterisk denote recipes which are demonstrated on RTE's *Simply Delicious Fish* television series.

Foreword

I first realised just how outstanding Irish fish actually is when I went on a foodie trip to Italy a few years ago. One of the highlights of the week was to be a visit to a very famous fish restaurant in Cesenatico on the Adriatic coast. We arrived full of anticipation, and the special meal prepared for us delighted my companions but left me with a blinding flash of realisation that the flavour of the fish was nothing like as good as what I took for granted every day in Ballycotton. I wished I could scoop everybody up and bring them home to taste it.

I came back fired with a new zeal for Irish fish which I have never lost. I have wanted to write a fish book ever since, but I'm glad I waited until now. At last in this country we are overcoming our prejudice against fish, which was for so long considered a Friday penance. Food scares, cholesterol warnings and concern about additives have all focussed attention on the fact that fish is healthy. Foreign travel and a more adventurous approach to cooking have introduced more people to it, also.

Although we still don't eat nearly enough fish in Ireland, I am heartened to see new fish counters appearing in supermarkets, and to find that the variety of seafood available around the country is steadily improving.

At the same time, a few depressing fishy facts have to be faced. For one thing, the condition of the fish on sale in many Irish shops still leaves a lot to be desired. 'Fresh' fish is often soggy and so many times defrosted that it's little wonder customers who try it don't come rushing back for more. The other perturbing thing I discovered when I worked behind the counter of a local fish shop as preparation for *Simply Delicious Fish* is that so many people only fry or, perish the thought, *boil* the fish they buy. Even more baffling to me were the customers who simply asked for 'a pound of boiling fish'. What on earth was I supposed to give them?

My other on-the-spot research involved going out with local fishermen and doing everything from baiting lobster pots to hauling in nets. Luckily for me the weather was good, but I realised more acutely than ever how tough a job fishing can be, especially in bad weather. Maybe if everybody stopped to think for a second about the hard labour that goes into landing our catches, fish would be treated with the care it deserves. It reminds me of the way my husband feels about vegetables. If people thought hard about the months of work that go into producing those, they wouldn't dream of boiling them to death!

Mention of vegetables brings me to another point about fish which is often completely overlooked. We must train ourselves to think in seasons and look forward to the different kinds of fish in the same way that we anticipate new potatoes or blackberries. There's all the difference in the world between eating a meltingly tender plaice in summer and a watery roe-filled one in January. The variation in flavour can be so dramatic that it's hard to believe you are actually eating the same fish. The same applies to many other fish and shellfish, so it's well worth noting the seasons as you go through the book.

If you are not already a fish lover as I am, I hope that *Simply Delicious Fish* will convert you. I would like to think that everybody in Ireland could regularly enjoy the luscious seafood we have all around us. At the same time I believe it is vital that we treat the sea's harvest with respect. I long for a situation where all fishermen will have the foresight to realise that we cannot go on scooping up fish indiscriminately from the bottom of the ocean. Our future stocks are being squandered. This makes it all the more essential for the government to safeguard the future of the fishing industry by giving the regional fisheries boards the resources and support they require. I would dearly like to see a new awareness of the need to protect our rivers and lakes and their precious fish stocks, too. What a goldmine to entice tourists into the very heart of the country! While in many places this had been drastically undervalued, in others its potential has actually been destroyed.

I have a dream that in every little fishing village in Ireland one could find a small seafood restaurant with no set menu but serving the fresh catch landed by the boats each day—maybe periwinkles, or succulent lobster, or spanking fresh plaice and chips. Everyone from pop stars to the local postman could sit happily side by side at simple gingham-clothed tables, as they do in port restaurants on the Continent, and tuck into a feast of Irish fish!

Acknowledgments

Once again I pay tribute to my mother-in-law Myrtle Allen who never fails to inspire me by her encyclopaedic knowledge and her generosity of spirit. It was she who really taught me through example the deep respect I now hold for good Irish ingredients. Many of the recipes in this fish book are hers and are favourites from the Ballymaloe restaurant menu which she has given me permission to share with you.

I would also like to thank my patient and very able team of teachers and assistants at the Ballymaloe Cookery School who tested and retested recipes until they couldn't look another fish straight in the eye—Florrie Cullinane, Fionnuala Ryan, Greg Dawson, Dervilla O'Flynn and Breda Fitzgerald.

My thanks also to my secretaries Rosalie Dunne and Adrienne Morrissey who deserve a very special mention. Adrienne actually postponed her summer holidays to type the manuscript for this book and indeed has worked late into the night with me on many occasions, for which I am truly grateful.

My *Simply Delicious* television crew once again deserve the highest praise for the constant support they gave me during the long, hot, stressful weeks of filming. Colette Farmer, my producer/director, cameramen Roy Bedell and Nick Dolan, soundmen Michael Cassidy and John Rogers, sparks Sean Keville and production assistant Mary Power all kept their heads when I was losing mine. Several of these lovely people have worked with me on all four series and have now become firm friends. I would like them to realise what a comfort it is for me to work with familiar faces, and long may they keep coming back for more.

I also want to say at this point how grateful I am that RTE have given me the opportunity to make these cookery programmes. It gives me tremendous joy and satisfaction to share my recipes, and the response to the programmes has been beyond my wildest dreams.

A special mention also for my very talented chef-brother Rory O'Connell, who not only gave me permission to use several of his delicious Ballymaloe recipes, but was also responsible for the inspired food styling both for the television series and for the photographs in the book. These were taken once again by Des Gaffney whose skill and conscientiousness I greatly admire.

I would particularly like to pay tribute to everybody at Bord Iascaigh Mhara for the exceptional work they have done over the years to make us all more aware of the wonderful variety of fish we have and for suggesting so many delicious ways to cook it. They were especially helpful to me while I was assembling information for this book.

I also want to thank my indulgent publisher Michael Gill, and my editor Mary Dowey who had the unhappy task of forcing me to shrink my considerable collection of fish recipes down to less than ninety for this book.

All along, my father-in-law Ivan Allen has been there gently nudging me forward to accept new challenges as they have come along and I have always been tremendously grateful for his and Myrtle's unstinting support.

And how could I forget my husband Tim, who was the first person to cook me a delectable piece of really fresh fish. It was love at first sight!

Buying Fresh Fish

Fresh is the only way to eat fish and that's that, so it's absolutely vital to be able to judge accurately whether fish is fresh or not. You sure as hell can't trust your fishmonger and you can't blame him either: he is dealing with a very perishable product and occasionally needs to have some dummies on whom he can pawn off stale fish, otherwise he'd go broke. Just make sure it's not you!

So let me give you a bit of advice on what to look out for. Fresh fish looks bright, slippery and lively—and not at all dull. The white underskin of flat fish should be really white and not yellowing. Stale fish really looks miserable. The eyes will be sunken and the skin can be gritty and dry and sometimes shiny, with a strong fishy smell. That's straightforward enough, but between the time fish is really fresh and the time it is really stale there are several days during which it will be gradually deteriorating. It is in this period that it's difficult to tell just what condition it is in, particularly if the fish has been cut into small pieces. You have to judge by the colour and smell. White fish should be white and the best thing of all to remember is that fresh fish doesn't smell fishy—it just has the merest scent of the sea, reminiscent of fresh seaweed.

It is well worthwhile building up a good relationship with your fishmonger, just as you do with your butcher. Ask for help and take the opportunity to learn every time you go shopping. When you get some delicious fresh fish remember to say how much you enjoyed it, but on the other hand if you get stale fish, hand it back gently but firmly, reminding your fishmonger that he or she must have known perfectly well that it wasn't fresh when they sold it to you.

For those who live far from the sea, frozen fish fillets can be excellent. Good firms freeze their fish within hours of it being caught, so it is far preferable to fresh fish several days old.

Glossary

Bain marie (or water bath): Can be any deep container, half-filled with hot water, in which delicate foods, e.g. custards or fish mousses, are cooked in their moulds or terrines. The bain marie is put into a low or moderate oven and the food is protected from direct heat by the gentle, steamy atmosphere, without risk of curdling. The term bain marie is also used for a similar container which holds several pans to keep soups, vegetables or stews warm during restaurant service.

Balsamic vinegar: A special old vinegar made in Modena in northeast Italy, aged slowly in oak casks so that it gradually becomes more concentrated. It must be at least 10 years old before it is sold, and is now beginning to appear in our shops. It is rare and expensive—well worth searching for.

Blanch: This cooking term can be confusing because it's used in many different senses. Usually it means to immerse food in water and to bring to the boil, parcook, extract salt or to loosen skins as in the case of almonds.

Bouquet garni: A small bunch of fresh herbs used to flavour stews, casseroles, stocks or soups, usually consisting of parsley stalks, a sprig of thyme, perhaps a bay leaf and an outside stalk of celery. Remove before serving.

Clingfilm (or 'Saran Wrap' as it is called in the United States): Used for sealing food from the air. Use 'pure' clingfilm or 'Glad Wrap'. Clingfilm containing PVC is considered harmful in contact with food.

Collop: A word sometimes used to describe pieces of monkfish or lobster tail, usually round in shape and about $\frac{1}{4}$ inch (5mm) thick unless otherwise stated.

Concassé: Concassé means roughly chopped, usually applied to tomatoes. Pour boiling water over very firm, ripe tomatoes, leave for 10 seconds, then pour off the water. Peel off the skin, cut in half, remove the seeds with a teaspoon or melon-baller, cut in quarters and chop into $\frac{1}{4}$ inch (5 mm) or $\frac{1}{8}$ inch (3 mm) dice. Concassé may be added to a sauce or used as a garnish.

Egg wash: A raw egg beaten with a pinch of salt, it is brushed on raw tarts, pies and biscuits to give them a shiny, golden glaze when cooked.

Grill pan: A heavy round or rectangular cast iron pan with a ridged bottom. The ridges mark the food attractively while keeping the fish or meat from direct contact with the fat. A heavy pan gives a good even heat — we use it for all pan-grilled fish.

Mezzaluna: A two-handled chopping knife with a round blade, used a lot in Italy.

Quenelle: Usually refers to an exquisitely light fish dumpling shaped with spoons into three-sided ovals.

Reduce: To boil down a liquid in an uncovered saucepan to concentrate the flavour. This is a very important technique in sauce-making.

Roux: Many of the sauces in this book call for roux. Roux is a basic liaison of butter and flour which is used as a thickening agent. Use equal quantities. Melt the butter, stir in the flour and cook on a low heat for 2 minutes, stirring occasionally. Roux can be stored in a covered bowl and used as required. It will keep for approx. 2 weeks in a refrigerator. 3 ozs (90 g/$\frac{1}{4}$ cup) of roux will thicken 1 pint (600 ml/$2\frac{1}{2}$ cups) of liquid. The liquid should be boiling as you whisk in the roux, otherwise it won't thicken properly. Roux is tremendously useful to have ready prepared in your kitchen and it will keep in a fridge for several weeks.

Seasoned flour: Plain white flour which has been seasoned with salt and freshly ground pepper. Fish for frying is usually coated in seasoned flour.

Sherry vinegar: A rich dark vinegar made from sherry and fermented in oak casks.

Sweat: To cook vegetables in a little fat or oil over a gentle heat in a covered saucepan, until they are almost soft but not coloured.

N.B. All Imperial spoon measurements in this book are rounded measurements unless the recipe states otherwise. All American spoon measurements are level.

Soups

I used to have a major mental block about making fish soups. Every recipe I read seemed to have an endless list of ingredients and a dauntingly complicated method. I've since discovered that with a few simple techniques fish soups are no more difficult to master than any other kind — yet they always look exciting. When you bring a fragrant fish soup to the table with tempting little bits of shellfish peeping out, it certainly seems much more exotic than spud soup (not that spud soup isn't delicious too!). Almost any fish can be used to produce wonderful soups of all sorts, from substantial chowders to light Chinese broths. Be sure to use good homemade fish stock if you possibly can. It's surprisingly quick and easy to make using either of the recipes here.

Basic Fish Stock

Makes 3 pints (1.7L/7$\frac{1}{2}$ cups) approx

Fish stock takes only 20 minutes to make. If you can get lots of nice fresh fish bones from your fishmonger it's well worth making 2 or 3 times this stock recipe, because it freezes perfectly and then you will have fish stock at the ready for any recipe that needs it.

$\frac{1}{4}$–$\frac{1}{2}$ oz (8–15 g/$\frac{1}{2}$ to 1 American tablesp.) butter
3$\frac{1}{2}$ ozs (100 g/scant 1 cup) onions, finely sliced
2$\frac{1}{4}$ lbs (1.01 kg) fish bones, preferably sole, turbot *or* brill
4–8 fl ozs (120–250 ml/$\frac{1}{2}$–1 cup) dry white wine

cold water to cover bones
4 peppercorns
bouquet garni containing a sprig of thyme, 4–5 parsley stalks, small piece of celery and a tiny scrap of bay leaf
no salt

Chop the fish bones into pieces and wash thoroughly under cold running water until no trace of blood remains. In a large stainless steel saucepan melt the butter, add the onions and sweat them on a gentle heat until soft but not coloured. Add the bones to the saucepan, stir and cook very briefly with the onions. Add the dry white wine and boil until nearly all the wine has evaporated. Cover with cold water, add the peppercorns and a large bouquet garni. Bring to the boil and simmer for 20 minutes, skimming often. Strain. Allow to get cold and refrigerate.

1

Demi-glaze

Reduce the strained fish stock by half to intensify the flavour, chill and refrigerate or freeze.

Glace de poisson

Reduce the stock until it becomes thick and syrupy, then chill. It will set into a firm jelly which has a very concentrated fish flavour— excellent to add to fish sauces or soup to enhance the flavour.

Household Fish Stock

Makes 4 pints (2.3L/10 cups) approx

This fish stock will be slightly darker in colour and stronger in flavour but excellent for fish soups and most sauces.

4 lbs (1.8 kg) bones, head and skin (gills removed) of fresh fish (oily fish like mackerel and herring are not suitable)
1 large onion
1 carrot
$\frac{1}{2}$ oz (15 g/1 American tablesp.) butter
4–8 fl ozs (120–250 ml/$\frac{1}{2}$–1 cup) dry white wine
cold water
6–8 peppercorns
bouquet garni containing a sprig of thyme, 4–5 parsley stalks, small piece of celery and a tiny scrap of bay leaf
no salt

Chop the fish bones into pieces and wash thoroughly under cold running water until no trace of blood remains. Slice the onion and carrot finely. In a large stainless steel saucepan melt the butter, add the onion and carrot and sweat them on a gentle heat until soft but not coloured. Add the bones to the saucepan, stir and cook very briefly with the onions. Add the dry white wine and boil until nearly all the wine has evaporated. Cover with cold water, add the peppercorns and a large bouquet garni. Bring to the boil and simmer for 20 minutes, skimming often. Strain. Allow to get cold and refrigerate.

*Seafood Chowder

Serves 6

A chowder is a wonderfully substantial fish soup or indeed it could almost be classified as a stew. It is certainly a meal in itself and there are lots of variations on the theme.

2

$1\frac{1}{2}$ lbs (675 g) haddock, monkfish, winter cod *or* any other firm white fish (*or* a mixture), free of bones and skin

1 lb (450 g) mixed, cooked, shellfish e.g. mussels, clams, scallops, shrimps *or* prawns and the cooking liquor (see page 95)

1 tablesp. (1 American tablesp. + 1 teasp.) olive *or* sunflower oil

4 ozs (110 g) streaky bacon (rind removed), cut into $\frac{1}{4}$ inch (5 mm) dice (blanch if necessary)

6–8 ozs (170–225 g/$1\frac{1}{2}$–2 cups) onions, chopped

1 oz (30 g/2 American tablesp.) flour

$\frac{3}{4}$ pint (450 ml/scant 2 cups) homemade fish stock (see page 1) *or* as a last resort water

$\frac{3}{4}$ pint (450 ml/scant 2 cups) milk

bouquet garni made up of 6 parsley stalks, 2 sprigs of thyme and a bay leaf

6 medium sized potatoes, e.g. Golden Wonders, cut into $\frac{1}{4}$ inch (5 mm) dice

salt and freshly ground pepper

pinch of mace

pinch of cayenne pepper

$\frac{1}{4}$ pint (150 ml/generous $\frac{1}{2}$ cup) light cream

Garnish
parsley and chives

Heat the oil in a stainless steel saucepan and brown the bacon well until it is crisp and golden. Add the onion, cover and sweat for a few minutes over a low heat. Stir in the flour and cook for a couple of minutes more. Add the fish stock or water gradually, then the milk, bouquet garni and potatoes. Season well with salt, pepper, mace and cayenne. Cover and simmer until the potatoes are almost cooked (5–6 minutes).*

Meanwhile cut the fish into roughly 1 inch (2.5 cm) square pieces. Add the fish to the pot as soon as the tip of a knife will go through the potato. Simmer gently for 3 or 4 minutes, stir in the cream and add the shellfish and any liquor from opening the mussels or clams. When the soup returns to the boil remove from the heat. Remember that the fish will continue to cook in the heat of the chowder so it should not be overcooked. Taste, correct seasoning and sprinkle with freshly chopped parsley and chives. Crusty hot white bread or hot crackers are usually served with a chowder.

*May be prepared ahead to this point.

Note: One could use about 4 oz (110 g) smoked haddock in this recipe. Poach it gently in some of the milk first and flake, then add to the chowder with the shellfish.

Mediterranean Fish Soup with Rouille

Serves 6–8

Fish soups can be made with all sorts of combinations of fish. Don't be the least bit bothered if you haven't got exactly the fish I suggest, but use a combination of whole fish and shellfish. The crab adds almost essential richness in my opinion.

$5\frac{1}{2}$ lbs (2.5 kg) mixed fish—e.g. 1 whole plaice, $\frac{1}{2}$ cod, 2 small whiting
3 swimming crab *or* 1 common crab, 6–8 mussels, 8–10 shrimps *or* prawns
5 fl ozs (150 ml/generous $\frac{1}{2}$ cup) olive oil
10 ozs (285 g/$2\frac{1}{2}$ cups) approx. onion, chopped
1 large clove garlic, crushed

5 large very ripe tomatoes *or* 1 × 14 oz (400 g) tin tomatoes
5 sprigs of fennel
2 sprigs of thyme
1 bay leaf
fish stock or water to cover (see page 1)
$\frac{1}{4}$ teasp. saffron
salt and freshly ground pepper
pinch of cayenne

Rouille

Serves 8

1 piece of French baguette bread, 2 inches (5 cm) approx.
6 tablesp. (8 American tablesp.) hot fish soup
4 cloves garlic

1 egg yolk, preferably free range
pinch of whole saffron stamens
salt and freshly ground pepper
6 tablesp. (8 American tablesp.) Extra Virgin olive oil

Garnish
chopped parsley

Croûtons
8 slices French bread
3–4 ozs (85–110 g) Gruyère cheese, grated

Cut the fish into chunks, bones, head and all (remove gills first). Heat the olive oil until smoking, add garlic and onions, toss for a minute or two, add the sliced tomatoes, herbs and fish including shells, cook for 10 minutes, then add enough fish stock or water to cover. Bring to a fast boil and cook for a further 10 minutes. Add more liquid if it reduces too much.

Soak the saffron strands in a little fish stock. Pick out the mussel shells. Taste, add salt, freshly ground pepper, cayenne, saffron and soaking liquid. Push the soup through a mouli (this may seem like an impossible task but you'll be surprised how effective it will be—there will be just a mass of dry bones left which you discard).

Next make the rouille. Cut the bread into cubes and soak in some hot fish soup. Squeeze out the excess liquid and mix to a mush in a bowl. Crush the garlic to a fine paste in a pestle and mortar, add the egg yolk, the saffron and the soggy bread. Season with salt and freshly ground pepper. Mix well and add in the oil drip by drip as in making mayonnaise. If the mixture looks too thick or oily add 2 tablespoons of hot fish soup and continue to stir.

Make the croûtons. Toast slices of French bread slowly until they are dry and crisp. Spread croûtons with rouille and sprinkle with Gruyère cheese. Bring the soup back to the boil and float a croûton in each plate of Mediterranean fish soup.

Cockle and Mussel Soup

Serves 10–12

Molly Malone, after whom the song was called, was a famous Dublin fishmonger. Among other things she sold, 'cockles and mussels, alive, alive-o'.

4–5 lbs (1.8–2.3 kg) mussels	2 sprigs of fresh fennel
4–5 lbs (1.8–2.3 kg) cockles	2 sprigs of fresh thyme
$\frac{3}{4}$ pint (450 ml/scant 2 cups) dry white wine	1 clove garlic, mashed
	freshly ground pepper
8 tablesp. (10 American tablesp. approx.) shallots, chopped	1–2 pints (600 ml–1.2L/$2\frac{1}{2}$–5 cups) boiling milk
10 sprigs of parsley	a little cream (optional)
$\frac{1}{2}$ fresh bay leaf	

Roux
2 ozs (55 g/$\frac{1}{2}$ stick) butter   2 ozs (55 g/scant $\frac{1}{2}$ cup) flour

Garnish
tiny crisp croûtons
finely chopped parsley

Wash the cockles and mussels in several changes of cold water checking that they are all tightly shut. Put the wine, shallots, parsley,

5

bay leaf, thyme, fennel and garlic into a wide stainless steel saucepan and add the cockles and mussels. Cover and cook over a gentle heat for a few minutes, stir frequently and as soon as the shells start to open pick them out. Remove the cockles and mussels from their shells and keep in a bowl.

Strain the cooking liquid and reduce it over a high heat to concentrate the flavour; taste frequently while it boils to make sure it is not too salty. Thicken with roux (see glossary for method), then thin out to a light consistency with the boiling milk. (If the milk is not brought to boiling point the acid in the wine will cause it to curdle.)

Taste for seasoning. Just before serving heat the soup, add a little cream and put some or all of the cockles and mussels back in.* Serve in old-fashioned soup plates with a sprinkling of chopped parsley on top. Serve tiny crisp croûtons separately (see below).

Note: If you have cockles and mussels left over, use for a salad or gratin (see page 90).

Croûtons for soup

Serves 8–12

> 2 slices slightly stale sliced
>   bread, $\frac{1}{4}$ inch (5 mm) thick
> 1 oz (30 g/$\frac{1}{4}$ stick) butter
>
> 2 tablesp. (2 American tablesp.
>   + 2 teasp.) olive oil

First cut the crusts off the bread, then cut into $\frac{1}{4}$ inch (5 mm) strips and then into exact cubes.

Melt the butter in a clean frying pan with the olive oil. Turn up the heat and add the croûtons. The pan should be quite hot at first, then reduce the heat to medium and *keep tossing all the time* until the croûtons are golden brown all over. Drain on kitchen paper.

Note: Croûtons can be made several hours or even a day ahead.

*Chinese Fish Soup with Spring Onions

Serves 6

I adore these light fish soups. Use this recipe as a formula and vary the fish and shellfish depending on what you have available—mussels and white crab meat are particularly delicious. You might even add some fresh chilli and lots of fresh coriander.

8 ozs (225 g) lemon sole *or* plaice
fillets, skinned
18 prawns *or* shrimps, cooked
and peeled
1 iceberg lettuce heart

2 pints (1.1 L/5 cups) very well
flavoured Chinese stock (see
below)
salt and lots of freshly ground
white pepper

Garnish
6 teasp. spring onion (scallion),
finely sliced at an angle

fresh coriander *or* flat parsley
prawn *or* shrimp roe if available

Cut the fish fillets into pieces about 1½ inches (4 cm) square. Shred the lettuce heart very finely. Bring the stock to the boil, add the salt and fish slices. Simmer for 1 minute. Add the prawns or shrimps and allow to heat through. Put 2 tablespoons (2 American tablesp. + 2 teasp.) of the shredded lettuce into each Chinese soup bowl, add plenty of white pepper and immediately ladle the boiling soup over it. Garnish with spring onions, prawns or shrimp roe and lots of fresh coriander. Serve very hot.

Basic Chinese Stock

Makes 3½ pints (2 litres) approx.

This delicious light but full flavoured stock is essential for Chinese fish or meat soups.

2 lbs (900 g) chicken pieces—
wings, drumsticks, necks etc.
2 lbs (900 g) pork spare ribs (*or*
total of 4 lbs/1.8 kg either
chicken pieces *or* ribs)
6 × ½ inch (1 cm) thick slices
fresh ginger root, unpeeled

3–4 large spring onions
(scallions)
8–10 pints (4.5–5.7 L/20–25 cups)
cold water
4 tablesp. (5 American tablesp.
+ 1 teasp.) Shao Hsing rice
wine

Tie the spring onion in knots like a real Chinese chef! Put all the ingredients in a large saucepan and cover with cold water. Bring to the boil and skim off any scum. Reduce the heat, cover and simmer gently for 4 hours approx., skimming regularly. Add the rice wine 5 minutes before the end of the cooking time. Strain the stock, cool, then refrigerate.

Remove the solidified fat from the top of the stock before use. The stock will keep in the refrigerator for at least a week; after that boil it every 2 or 3 days. It also freezes perfectly.

Plaice, Lemon Sole, Dab, Flounder and Megrim

Plaice best June–October
Lemon sole best July–November
Dab best October–February
Flounder best June–October
Megrim best October–February

As children, we were always thrilled when fillets of plaice arrived on the bus from Dublin on a Thursday evening. My mother cooked them very simply in a little bit of butter on the pan and they were delicious. When I arrived in Shanagarry plaice was the first fish I tasted fresh from the sea and it was a complete revelation to me. Suddenly I understood why people wax lyrical about really fresh fish in season.

The various members of the extensive flat fish family are widely available and each has a quite distinctive flavour. They vary considerably in price, and occasionally one is passed off as another, so it is important to be able to recognise them. Some of the cheapest actually taste best.

All white fish should be bright and slippery in appearance with white, not discoloured, skin underneath.

Plaice has bright orange spots and a very smooth skin.

Lemon sole is similar in shape and has smooth skin also, but it does not have spots. It should not be considered the poor relation of plaice.

Dab has barely discernible spots and darker, rougher skin. It is substantially cheaper and well worth looking out for.

Flounder has rough spikes down the centre of its back, and a very dark skin on top with very white skin underneath.

Megrim (also called white sole) is very pale—almost transparent—and looks slightly more cross-eyed than the other flatfish. It is not held in very high regard in Ireland, but the Spanish are very fond of it and prepared to pay a high price for it.

The recipes in this section can be used for any flat fish, but obviously the flavour will vary depending on the type used.

Baked Plaice with Chanterelles

Serves 4 as a main course

Chanterelles are in season from July to the end of September. We get ours from the old pine woods on the Beara Peninsula in West Cork. Baked plaice with chanterelles can be served as a first course or as a main course, depending on the size of the fish. If chanterelles aren't available just serve the plaice with the herb butter.

4 very fresh plaice on the bone
salt and freshly ground pepper
8 ozs (225 g) fresh chanterelles
2–4 ozs (55–110 g/½–1 stick) butter

4 teasp. fresh parsley *or* **a**
mixture of parsley, chives,
fennel and lemon thyme
leaves, finely chopped

Preheat the oven to 190°C/375°F/regulo 5.

Turn the fish on to its side and remove the head. Wash the fish and clean the slit very thoroughly. With a sharp knife, cut through the skin right around the fish, just where the 'fringe' meets the flesh. Be careful to cut neatly and to join the side cuts at the tail or it will be difficult to remove the skin later on.

Sprinkle the fish with salt and pepper and lay them in $\frac{1}{4}$ inch (5 mm) of water in a shallow baking tin. Bake in the preheated oven for 20–30 minutes according to the size of the fish. The water should have just evaporated as the fish is cooked. Check to see if the fish is ready by lifting the flesh from the bone at the head: it should lift off easily and be quite white with no trace of pink.

Pick over the chanterelles carefully and cut off the tough end bits. Wash quickly, drain on absorbent paper and cut into pieces. Melt $\frac{1}{2}$ oz (15 g/$\frac{1}{8}$ stick) butter and when it foams toss in the chanterelles and season with salt and freshly ground pepper. Cook on high heat for 3–4 minutes or until soft.

Melt the remaining butter and stir in the freshly chopped herbs and chanterelles. Just before serving, catch the skin of the plaice down near the tail and pull off gently (the skin will tear badly if not properly cut). Lift the fish on to hot plates and spoon the herb butter and chanterelles over it. Serve immediately.

Note: All flat fish are delicious cooked in this way, e.g. black sole, lemon sole, brill, turbot, dab and flounder. The sauce can be varied— Hollandaise, Mousseline, Beurre blanc, Lobster and Champagne Sauce are all very good.

*Plaice or Sole Bonne Femme

Serves 6–8 as a main course, 12–16 as a starter

A wickedly rich and delicious recipe by anybody's standards. Don't bother to make it unless you are prepared to put in the butter and cream that the recipe calls for, because that, I'm sad to tell you, is why it tastes so exquisite!

5–6 lbs (2.3–2.7 kg) plaice or
  Dover sole (this will yield
  $2\frac{1}{2}$–3 lbs (1.12–1.35 kg) fillets
  approx.

Fish stock

bones from the fish and skins
  too if you like
$\frac{1}{4}$–$\frac{1}{2}$ oz (8–15 g/$\frac{1}{2}$–1 tablesp.) butter
1 onion, thinly sliced
8 fl ozs (225 ml/1 cup) dry white
  wine

4 *or* 5 peppercorns
a bouquet garni consisting of 3
  or 4 parsley stalks, a sprig of
  thyme, a small piece of celery
  and a tiny scrap of bay leaf
no salt

1 oz (30 g/$\frac{1}{4}$ stick) butter
$\frac{1}{2}$–$\frac{3}{4}$ lb (225–340 g/4–5 cups) very
  fresh white mushrooms, thinly
  sliced

salt and freshly ground pepper
squeeze of lemon juice
Duchesse potato (see page 27)

tiny scrap of butter
1 tablesp. (1 American tablesp.
  + 1 teasp.) shallots, finely
  chopped
salt and freshly ground pepper

2 tablesp. (2 American tablesp.
  + 2 teasp.) approx. roux (see
  glossary)
$\frac{1}{4}$ pint (150 ml/$\frac{1}{2}$ cup) milk

Liaison

2 egg yolks
$\frac{1}{4}$ pint (150 ml/$\frac{1}{2}$ cup) cream

2–4 ozs (55–110 g/$\frac{1}{2}$–1 stick) butter

First fillet and skin the fish, wash the bones well under cold running water and then make the fish stock. Melt the butter and sweat the onion gently for a few minutes, add the bones to the saucepan, stir and cook very briefly with the onions. Add the dry white wine and boil until nearly all the wine has evaporated. Add cold water to cover, peppercorns and a large bouquet garni. Bring to the boil and skim; simmer for 20 minutes, skimming often. Strain.

Meanwhile melt the butter in a frying pan, cook the sliced mushrooms in batches in a very hot pan, season with salt and freshly ground pepper and a squeeze of lemon juice and keep warm. Pipe a border of Duchesse potato around a serving dish.

Butter a wide saucepan very meanly (I use a 9 inch/23 cm stainless steel sauté pan with a lid) and sprinkle with half the shallots. Fold in the ends of the fish fillets and lay them on top of the shallots in a single layer, sprinkle the remainder of the shallots over the top, season with freshly ground pepper and a little salt. Pour over just enough strained fish stock to cover the fillets, bring to the boil and poach gently for 5–6 minutes or until the fish is almost cooked through. This can be done in an oven preheated to 230°C/450°F/regulo 8, or on a very low heat on top of the stove. Cooking time depends on the size and thickness of the fillets. Sole takes longer to cook than plaice and both seem to take longer in the oven than on top, sometimes up to 10 minutes. However it's really easy to overcook the fish at this point, so err on the side of having it underdone.

When the fish is just cooked remove it to a plate. Put the Duchesse potato into a moderate oven to heat. Strain the cooking liquid and reduce to $\frac{3}{4}$ pint (450 ml) over a medium heat. Thicken with roux, then add milk and boil for a minute or two.

Make a liaison by whisking the egg yolks and cream together in a bowl. Pour some of the hot sauce into the liaison, whisk well and mix this with the remainder of the sauce in the saucepan, return to the heat and simmer for 1 minute. Check seasoning, finally remove from the heat and whisk in the butter in little bits. Then add the cooked mushrooms to the sauce and check seasoning again.

Arrange the fish fillets on the hot serving dish in the centre of the Duchesse potato. Spoon the sauce over the fish. Put into a moderate oven, 180°C/350°F/regulo 4, to heat through and flash under the grill for a minute to brown the top if necessary.

Note: Plaice or Sole Bonne Femme may be served as a starter in scallop shells or individual dishes or it may be served as a main course. All flat fish may be cooked by this technique.

Sole à la Dieppoise is a variation on the recipe above. Add 3 lbs (1.35 kg) mussels and $\frac{1}{2}$ lb (225 g) cooked shelled prawns or shrimps to the recipe instead of the mushrooms.

Goujons of Plaice, Sole or Monkfish

Serves 6–8 as a main course

Goujons are narrow little strips of fish fillet cut across the grain, more or less the size of a fresh water gudgeon. They are usually dipped in batter and deepfried but can be also dipped in milk and seasoned flour. Either way, this is a very good recipe to make a little fish go a long way.

6–8 skinned fillets of sole *or* **plaice** *or* **1–2 medium-sized monkfish tails**

olive or **sunflower oil for deep-frying**

Batter
5 ozs (140 g/1 cup) plain flour
1$\frac{3}{4}$ tablesp. (2 American tablesp. + 1 teasp.) olive oil

1–1$\frac{1}{2}$ egg whites
sea salt

Garnish
segments of lemon

parsley

Accompaniment
Tartare sauce (see page 46), Orly sauce (see page 13) *or* Garlic Mayonnaise (below)

First make the batter. Sieve the flour into a bowl, make a well in the centre, pour in the olive oil, stir and add enough water to make a batter about the consistency of double cream. Allow to stand for at least 1 hour.

Cut the sole or plaice into $\frac{1}{2}$ inch (1 cm) strips on the bias. Heat the oil in the deep fryer to very hot, 200°C/400°F. Just before serving, whisk the egg whites to a stiff peak and fold into the batter, adding a good pinch of sea salt. Dip each goujon individually into the batter and drop them into the hot oil. Fry until golden – 1–2 minutes approx. Drain on kitchen paper and serve on a hot plate with a tiny bowl or oyster shell full of sauce in the centre. Garnish with a segment of lemon and a sprig of parsley.

Garlic Mayonnaise
homemade mayonnaise (for ingredients and method see page 64)

1–4 cloves garlic depending on the size
2 teasp. chopped parsley

Crush the garlic and add to the egg yolks just as you start to make the mayonnaise. Finally add the chopped parsley and taste for seasoning.

Plaice or Sole à l'Orly

Serves 3–4 as a main course, 6–8 as a starter

In this recipe, whole fillets of fish rather than strips are deepfried, and Orly sauce is another variation on the mayonnaise theme.

6–8 fillets of very fresh plaice *or* **sole, skinned**
batter (see above)

6–8 small ripe tomatoes (optional)

Garnish
chervil *or* **flat parsley**

segments of lemon

Orly sauce
4 tablesp. (5 American tablesp. approx.) homemade mayonnaise (see page 64)

½–1 teasp. concentrated tomato purée

Mix the tomato purée with the mayonnaise, taste and correct seasoning if necessary.

Heat the oil to hot, 200°C/400°F. Just before serving fold the egg whites into the batter, dip each fillet of fish individually and fry until crisp and golden. Serve on a hot plate with Orly sauce. We sometimes hollow out a tiny tomato for each person and fill it with the sauce. Garnish with sprigs of parsley or chervil and a segment of lemon on each plate.

Dover or Black Sole

Best October–May

Long considered one of the very finest fish, Dover sole (often referred to as black sole in Ireland) is highly regarded by restaurateurs, and for good reason. Unlike many fish, it actually improves in texture when kept for a day or so, and it has a very high ratio of flesh to bone. Its light frame makes a wonderfully delicate fish stock.

Sole (whose name indicates that it is flat like the sole of the foot) is longer and slimmer than plaice; its rough skin, dark on top, white underneath, has tiny scales which must be removed. The skin can be pulled off in one piece—essential if you intend to cook it on the bone—but if you want to use fillets I think it is best to fillet it first and then skin it in the normal way.

Sole or Plaice à la Meunière

Serves 4 as a main course, 8 as a starter

A classic way to cook fish, but deceptively simple. Heat control is vital and it is only worth doing if the fish is absolutely fresh.

8 perfect fillets of very fresh fish	**seasoned flour (see glossary)**
clarified butter (see below)	**squeeze of lemon juice**

Garnish

sprigs of chervil *or* parsley	**lemon segments**

Skin the fillets. Choose a wide, heavy frying pan and melt a few tablespoons of clarified butter in it. Coat the fillets lightly in seasoned flour, put skin side upwards into the pan in a single layer, cook on that side without turning until golden, then flip over to cook the second side. Stand over the pan adjusting the heat as necessary but resist the temptation to keep turning the fish over and over or you will not get the fillets perfectly golden.

When cooked put the fillets skin side down on hot plates. Wipe out the pan, melt a little fresh butter, add a squeeze or two of fresh lemon juice and spoon a little of the buttery juices over each serving. Garnish each plate with a segment of lemon and a sprig of chervil or parsley and serve immediately.

Clarified Butter

Melt 8 ozs (225 g/2 sticks) of butter gently in a saucepan or in the oven, allow to stand for a few minutes, then spoon the crusty white layer of salt particles off the top of the melted butter. Underneath this crust there is clear liquid butter which is called clarified butter. The milky liquid at the bottom can be discarded or used in a Béchamel sauce.

Clarified butter is excellent for cooking because it can withstand a higher cooking temperature than normal butter. It will keep in the fridge for several weeks but must be covered.

Sole Stuffed with Prawns and Garlic Butter

Serves 4 as a main course

This recipe would be perfect for a 'slightly grand' dinner party, and most of the preparation can be done in advance. It is delicious with plaice and lemon sole also.

8 fillets of sole, each $2\frac{1}{2}$ ozs (70 g) approx.
2 tablesp. (2 American tablesp. + 2 teasp.) approx. garlic butter (see page 28)
salt and freshly ground pepper

16 large *or* 24 small cooked prawns (see page 72 for cooking method)
2–3 tablesp. (3–4 American tablesp.) homemade fish stock (see page 1)

Hollandaise sauce (see page 55)

Garnish
sprigs of chervil *or* fennel

Preheat the oven to 180°C/350°F/regulo 4.

Put the fillets skin side uppermost on the work surface, season with salt and freshly ground pepper and spread 1 teaspoon of garlic butter over each fillet. Put 2 or 3 cooked prawns on the narrow end of each fillet and roll up towards the wide end.

Put the rolled fillets on to a large pyrex or ovenproof plate, cover with tinfoil and tuck it in well underneath the plate. Bake in the preheated oven for 15–18 minutes, depending on the thickness of the fillets; the fish should be beautifully soft and moist.

Meanwhile, make a Hollandaise sauce (see page 55, omitting the cucumber). When the fish is cooked whisk in some or all of the cooking juices to make a light fluffy sauce. Pour a little sauce on to each individual hot plate. Place two fish rolls on top, garnish with sprigs of chervil or fennel and serve immediately.

Turbot or Brill

Best March–October

I dream about finding one of those wonderful diamond-shaped copper turbot kettles at an auction, all black and tarnished and so unrecognisable that I'd manage to buy it for half nothing. I would polish it up and dream next about having a whole turbot to poach in it, because there's no doubt that turbot is one of life's great pleasures. The flesh is firm, delicate and has an exquisite flavour, and even the bones are highly prized for a really fine fish stock. It can be cooked whole, filleted or cut into steaks. Brill sometimes suffers from being compared, usually unfavourably, to turbot. It is a delicious fish in its own right, even if it is slightly less firm-fleshed and not quite so delicate in flavour—it is, after all, much less expensive.

Turbot and brill, both flat fish, are similar in shape and size but turbot has a shorter, wider body, is slightly speckled and has rather knobbly skin on the dark side. I remember this by connecting 't' for turbot with 't' for thorns in my mind. Brill has completely smooth grey-brown skin on the upper side.

Turbot, Brill, Cod or Monkfish with Black Peppercorns

Serves 8 as a main course

This recipe for fish with peppercorns sounds most unlikely. It is an adaptation of a recipe in Jane Grigson's *Fish Book*, and even though it is a little extravagant it's certainly worth it for the delicious result.

8 turbot, brill, cod *or* monkfish steaks, 1 inch (5 mm) thick (allow about 5 ozs/140 g per person)
salt
1 heaped tablesp. (2 American tablesp.) whole black peppercorns
1½ tablesp. (2 American tablesp.) flour

Garnish
flat parsley *or* watercress sprigs

1½ ozs (45 g/⅜ stick) unsalted butter
1 tablesp. (1 American tablesp. + 1 teasp.) olive oil
2 fl ozs (50 ml/¼ cup) brandy
2 fl ozs (50 ml/¼ cup) port
¼ pint (150 ml/generous ½ cup) fish stock (see page 1) *or* light chicken stock
¼ pint (150 ml/generous ½ cup) cream

16

Season the fish steaks with salt. Crush the peppercorns coarsely in a pestle and mortar and mix with the flour. Coat the fish on both sides with this mixture. Melt $\frac{1}{2}$ oz (15 g/$\frac{1}{8}$ stick) butter with the olive oil in a wide frying pan and fry the steaks on a gentle heat until golden on both sides. When the fish is almost cooked add the brandy and port and flame, then add the stock, bring to the boil and simmer for 3–4 minutes or until the fish is just cooked through.

Lift the fish carefully on to a serving dish. Add the cream to the pan and reduce until the sauce thickens to a light coating consistency. Whisk in the last 1 oz (30 g/$\frac{1}{4}$ stick) butter. Taste and correct seasoning. Spoon over the fish and serve immediately. Garnish with flat parsley or watercress sprigs.

Note: This fish dish reheats surprisingly well.

Turbot or Brill with Carrot and Chives

Serves 6 as a main course

Another delicious recipe which I managed to extract out of my brother Rory O'Connell!

6 fillets turbot *or* **brill weighing 4–5 ozs (110–140 g) each**
$\frac{1}{2}$ oz (15 g/1 American tablesp.) butter

few sprigs of fennel
salt and freshly ground pepper

Carrot purée
1 lb (450 g) carrots
$\frac{1}{4}$ pint (150 ml/generous $\frac{1}{2}$ cup) water
salt and freshly ground pepper

pinch of sugar
1 oz (30 g/$\frac{1}{4}$ stick) butter
2 fl ozs (50 ml/$\frac{1}{4}$ cup) cream

Hollandaise sauce (see page 55)

Garnish
1 tablesp. (1 American tablesp. + 1 teasp.) chives, finely chopped

Wash the carrots and peel thinly if necessary. Bring the water to the boil. Cut the carrots in $\frac{1}{4}$ inch (5 mm) thick slices and add to the boiling water. Season with salt, pepper and a pinch of sugar. Cover and cook until soft. Remove the carrots with a perforated spoon, reserve the liquid, purée the carrots with the butter and cream, taste and correct seasoning.

Preheat the oven to 180°C/350°F/regulo 4. Bake the fish fillets in one large foil packet with fennel, salt and freshly ground pepper (it will take 10–15 minutes).

Meanwhile make the Hollandaise sauce by the usual method (see page 55, omitting the cucumber). Thin out the sauce by whisking in a little of the reserved carrot cooking liquid. Taste and season the sauce, adding more lemon juice if necessary; it should be the consistency of light pouring cream.

When the fish is cooked, remove the skin and lift each fillet on to a hot serving plate. Put 4 or 5 teaspoons of purée around each plate in 'quenelle' shapes (little ovals), coat the fish with the sauce, sprinkle a ring of finely chopped chives around each piece of fish and serve immediately.

Whiting

Best November–March

Many people have dreadful childhood memories of steamed fish on a Friday which they were told to eat up because it was good for them— and generally that fish was whiting. There is no reason at all why whiting, if it's carefully cooked, should have this dull image. I have several recipes for wonderfully warming family dishes, as well as an exquisite fish mousse. This underrated fish has the twin advantages of being widely available and tremendously good value.

Whiting is a small, round fish with a thin, silvery skin and a dark spot at the base of the pectoral fin. As with most fish, the flesh when fresh is white rather than creamy grey.

Whiting Baked in a Parsley Sauce

Serves 4 as a main course

4 fillets of very fresh whiting
salt and freshly ground pepper

tiny dab of butter

Parsley sauce
a few slices of carrot and onion
**a sprig of thyme and the stalks
   of the parsley (below)**
**1 pint (600 ml/2½ cups) rich milk
   or 18 fl ozs (scant 600 ml/2¼
   cups) milk and 2 fl ozs (50 ml/
   ¼ cup) cream**

roux (see glossary)
**4 tablesp. (5 American tablesp.
   + 1 teasp.) chopped parsley**
salt and freshly ground pepper

Topping
**2 ozs (55 g/¾ cup) buttered
   crumbs (see page 25)**

**1 dessertsp. (2 American teasp.)
   chopped parsley**

First make the parsley sauce. Put the carrot, onion, thyme and parsley stalks into the cold milk and bring slowly to the boil. Simmer for 3 or 4 minutes, turn off the heat and allow to infuse for 5 to 10 minutes. Strain the milk, return to the boil and whisk in enough roux to thicken the sauce to coating consistency. Add 3 tablespoons of chopped parsley and season with salt and freshly ground pepper. Reduce the heat to the absolute minimum or better still use a heat diffuser mat and barely simmer for 8–10 minutes.

Meanwhile remove the fins and any remaining bones from the whiting and season with salt and freshly ground pepper. Arrange in a single layer on a lightly buttered ovenproof dish. Add the remainder of the parsley to the sauce and spoon over the fish fillets to cover completely. Bake in a preheated moderate oven, 180°C/350°F/regulo 4, for 15–20 minutes. Sprinkle with buttered crumbs mixed with parsley and flash under the grill until crusty and golden. Serve immediately.

Variations on the theme

Whiting with Orange and Buttered Crumbs

Follow the recipe for Whiting Baked in a Parsley Sauce but add the grated rind of 1 orange to the sauce before coating the fish. Omit the parsley.

Whiting with Mushrooms

Follow the recipe for Whiting Baked in a Parsley Sauce but add 4 tablespoons of finely diced, well seasoned sautéed mushrooms to the sauce before coating the fish.

Whiting with Mangetouts, Carrots and Chervil

1½ lbs (675 g) whiting fillets *or* cod, pollock, mullet, salmon *or* trout
a little butter
4 ozs (110 g) mangetout peas
4 ozs (110 g) carrots, peeled and cut into ⅛ inch (3 mm) julienne strips

Beurre blanc (see page 81)
salt and pepper
1 dessertsp. (2 American teasp.) chopped chives
1 dessertsp. (2 American teasp.) chopped fennel

Garnish
sprigs of fresh chervil

Grey Sea Mullet with Gruyère and Mustard

Gratin of Cod with Bacon, Tomatoes and Dill

Plaice Bonne Femme

A Selection of Irish Shellfish with Homemade Mayonnaise

Hot Buttered Oysters

Cut the fish fillets into neat diamond shapes a little smaller than a match box. Place them on a lightly buttered baking sheet and season lightly with salt and freshly ground pepper. Sprinkle about 6 tablespoons of water over the fish to create a little steam when it is being cooked. Cook the vegetables in boiling salted water until barely cooked (they should still have a slight bite). Keep warm.

Meanwhile make the Beurre blanc (see page 81). Add chopped herbs to the sauce and keep it in a warm place until needed.

Preheat the oven to 200°C/400°F/regulo 6. Put the fish into the preheated oven and cook for 4–5 minutes depending on the type of fish being used. When the fish no longer looks opaque it is cooked. Remove from the oven and add any juices from the baking sheet to the Beurre blanc sauce. Add half the vegetables and chopped herbs to the sauce. Put the fish into a serving dish or divide equally between four plates. Coat the fish with the sauce and sprinkle the rest of the vegetables over the dish. Garnish with chervil and serve immediately.

Fish Mousse with Shrimp Butter Sauce

Serves 16–20 as a starter

This recipe makes a large number of light fish mousses. It's a favourite on our menu and can be served with many sauces. Even though the mousse is light it is also very rich, so it's vital to cook it in small ramekins. They can be done in several batches as the raw mixture keeps perfectly overnight, covered in a cold fridge. Cooked crab meat, oysters, prawns, periwinkles or a tiny dice of cucumber could be added to a Beurre blanc sauce to serve with them.

12 ozs (340 g) very fresh fillets of whiting *or* pollock, skinned and totally free of bone or membrane
1 teasp. salt
pinch of freshly ground white pepper
1 egg, preferably free range
1 egg white

generous 1¼ pints (750 ml/ generous 3 cups) cream, chilled
Beurre blanc sauce recipe × 2 (see page 81)
4–8 ozs (110–225 g) peeled cooked shrimps
¼ oz (8 g/½ tablesp.) butter

Garnish
sprigs of chervil

whole cooked shrimps (optional)

ramekins—2½ fl ozs (65 ml) capacity, 2 inches (5 cm) × 1 inch (2.5 cm) deep

21

Cut the whiting fillets into small dice, purée in the chilled bowl of a food processor, add the salt and freshly ground pepper and then add the egg and egg white and continue to purée until it is well incorporated. Rest and chill in the fridge for 30 minutes.

Meanwhile, line the ramekins with pure clingfilm or brush with melted butter. When the fish has rested for 30 minutes, blend in the cream and whizz again just until it is well incorporated. Check seasoning. Fill the mousse into the moulds and put them in a bain marie. Cover with a pricked sheet of tinfoil or greaseproof paper. Bring the water in the bain marie just to boiling point, put it in the oven at 200°C/400°F/regulo 6 and bake for 20–30 minutes. The mousses should feel just firm in the centre and will keep perfectly for 20–30 minutes in a plate-warming oven.

Meanwhile make the Beurre blanc sauce (see page 81) and keep warm. When the mousses are cooked remove them to a warm place and leave to rest. Toss the shrimps in a very little foaming butter until hot through, add them to the sauce, taste and correct seasoning: the sauce should be very thin and light. Pour a little hot sauce on to each plate, unmould a mousse, place it in the centre and garnish with shrimps and sprigs of fresh chervil.

Note: It is vital to season the raw mixture well, otherwise the mousse will taste bland.

Fish Mousse in Courgette Flowers

This is a very grand way of serving the fish mousse described above – the perfect way to make use of all the flowers if you grow your own courgettes.

allow 1 male flower per person   fish mousse (see above)

Prepare the flowers by removing the stamen and the tiny little thorns from the base. Drop the flowers into boiling salted water and immediately remove them and plunge them into a large bowl of iced water. Remove from the water and drain on kitchen paper. Fill the courgette flowers with the fish mousse (a piping bag with a plain nozzle is best for this fiddly operation).

Put them on a greased baking sheet which has been moistened with a little water, cover with tinfoil and bake in a preheated moderate oven, 180°C/350°F/regulo 4, for 15–20 minutes or until firm to the touch. Serve on hot plates with Beurre blanc sauce (see page 81).

Garnish with sprigs of chervil or fennel.

Cod, Haddock, Hake, Pollock and Ling

Best November–March

Of the various members of the round fish family, cod is by far the best known and best loved, but I'm afraid in my opinion it is one of the most overpriced fish in the sea. Having said that, however, I admit it can occasionally be very delicious and well worth the money when it is actually in season and very fresh, but too often it is flabby and flavourless. I avoid it in the summer because it's not at its best and seems to go off faster than any fish I know.

Other varieties of round fish can be better value and are worth experimenting with. The recipes in this section are suitable for all the round fish mentioned.

Cod has a smooth skin, usually flecked with yellowy gold, and a little 'smig' under its chin. Traditionally it was salted, and is still sold in this form in some places.

Haddock is darker skinned, with a thumb print of St Peter on its side. I find it very good fresh, but much of it goes for smoking, and too much of that seems to be dyed bright orange. I long for somebody to produce a traditional smoked Finnan haddock again.

Hake is a long fish with silvery skin and a vicious looking mouth full of teeth. It's a great favourite of mine.

Pollock (both black and white) is fatter, with rather rough charcoal-green skin. Its mild taste makes it popular with reluctant fish eaters. White pollock has a finer flavour than black.

Ling is long and slim — almost eel-like — with a completely smooth skin and a little 'smig' under the chin. It takes well to being dried and salted also.

Taramasalata

Serves 8–10 as a first course

A much abused recipe which should for perfection be made in a pestle and mortar, but I make a very passable version in a food processor. It only takes seconds and tastes infinitely more delicious that the alarming bright pink paste sometimes served up as Taramasalata in some continental restaurants.

4 ozs (110 g) smoked cod's roe
2 slices white bread
1 egg yolk
1 clove garlic, peeled and
    crushed

$\frac{1}{4}$–$\frac{1}{2}$ pint (150–300 ml/generous $\frac{1}{2}$ cup–1$\frac{1}{4}$ cups) sunflower or arachide oil mixed with a dash or two of olive oil
juice of $\frac{1}{2}$–1 freshly squeezed lemon

Garnish
black olives

Take the skin off the cod's roe and soak the roe in cold water for 15–30 minutes, depending on how salty it is. Drain well. Cut the crusts off the bread and soak the rest in a little water for a few minutes so that it can be made into a paste. (Squeeze out any excess liquid.) Put the egg yolk into the bowl of a food processor, add the garlic, soggy bread and smoked cod's roe, whizz for a few seconds then add the oil gradually as though you were making mayonnaise. Add freshly squeezed lemon juice to taste.

Serve chilled with black olives and crusty white bread or hot thin toast.

Note: Many taramasalata recipes call for olive oil but I find the flavour too strong, so I use a small proportion of olive oil with sunflower or arachide.

Gratin of Cod with Bacon, Tomatoes and Dill

Serves 4 as a main course

My RTE producer Colette Farmer deserves credit for this dish. She described it to me and we came up with this version which she pronounced Simply Delicious!

1$\frac{1}{4}$ lbs (560 g) cod fillets
4–6 ozs (110–170 g) streaky bacon
    rashers (rindless)
1 tablesp. (1 American tablesp.
    + 1 teasp.) olive oil
1 large onion, chopped (6 ozs/
    1$\frac{1}{2}$ cups approx.)
10 ozs (285 g) very ripe tomatoes,
    skinned, seeded, flesh cut into
    $\frac{1}{2}$ inch (1 cm) dice
salt and freshly ground pepper

pinch of sugar
1 dessertsp. (2 American teasp.)
    fresh dill or 1 tablesp. (1
    American tablesp. + 1 teasp.)
    or a mixture of parsley, chives,
    fennel and lemon thyme
$\frac{1}{2}$ oz (15 g/1 American tablesp.)
    butter
1 oz (30 g/scant $\frac{1}{2}$ cup) soft white
    breadcrumbs
4 ozs (110 g/1 cup) Gruyère or
    Cheddar cheese, grated

ovenproof dish $8\frac{1}{2}$ × 10 inches
(21.5 × 25.5 cm)

Cut the rashers into 1 inch (2.5 cm) pieces. Heat the olive oil in a pan, add the rashers, fry until crisp, remove and sprinkle over the base of the ovenproof dish. Sweat the onions in the oil and bacon fat for 5–8 minutes.

Meanwhile skin the fillets of fish, cut into 4 portions and season well with salt and freshly ground pepper. Put the onions on top of the rashers and arrange the fish fillets on top. Season the diced tomato flesh with salt, freshly ground pepper and sugar and add the herbs. Spread this over the fish, cover the whole dish with tinfoil and bake in a moderate oven, 180°C/350°F/regulo 4, for 30–40 minutes.

Meanwhile make the buttered crumbs. Melt the butter, stir in the crumbs, turn out on to a plate, cool and mix with the grated cheese. When the fish is cooked sprinkle with the topping and allow to brown under a preheated grill for 5 minutes approx. until crisp and golden.

Serve garnished with flat parsley.

Note: This recipe is also delicious with Mornay sauce (see page 26) as well as buttered crumbs.

Gratin of Cod with Buttered Leeks

Serves 6–8 as a main course

A master recipe which can be adapted in lots of different ways. You may even find it one of the most useful in the whole book.

2 lbs (900 g) cod fillets
1 lb (450 g) leeks, trimmed and sliced into $\frac{1}{4}$ inch (5 mm) thick rounds

1 oz (30 g/$\frac{1}{4}$ stick) butter
salt and freshly ground pepper
1 tablesp. (1 American tablesp. + 1 teasp.) water if necessary

Mornay sauce
1 pint (600 ml/2$\frac{1}{2}$ cups) milk
a few slices of carrot and onion
3 or 4 peppercorns
a sprig of thyme and parsley
2 ozs (55 g/$\frac{1}{3}$ cup) approx. roux (see glossary)
5–6 ozs (140–170 g/1$\frac{1}{4}$–1$\frac{1}{2}$ cups) grated Cheddar cheese *or* 3 ozs (85 g/$\frac{3}{4}$ cup) grated Parmesan cheese

$\frac{1}{4}$ teasp. mustard, preferably Dijon
salt and freshly ground pepper
1 tablesp. (1 American tablesp. + 1 teasp.) parsley, chopped (optional)

Buttered crumbs
1 oz (30 g/¼ stick) butter
2 ozs (55 g/scant 1 cup) soft
white breadcrumbs

To finish
1¾ lbs (790 g) approx. Duchesse
potato (optional, see below)

Wash the leeks well (just use the white and pale green part—darker green leaves can be added to a stock pot). Melt the butter in a heavy casserole; when it foams add the sliced leeks and toss gently to coat with butter. Season with salt and freshly ground pepper and add the water if necessary. Cover with a paper lid and the close-fitting lid of the saucepan. Reduce the heat and cook very gently for 15–30 minutes or until soft and moist.

Meanwhile make the Mornay sauce. Put the cold milk into a saucepan with the carrot and onion, peppercorns, thyme and parsley. Bring to the boil, simmer for 4–5 minutes, remove from the heat and leave to infuse for 10 minutes if you have enough time. Strain out the vegetables, bring the milk back to the boil and thicken with roux to a light coating consistency. Add the mustard and two thirds of the grated cheese; keep the remainder for sprinkling over the top. Season with salt and freshly ground pepper, taste and correct seasoning if necessary. Add the optional parsley.

Next make the buttered crumbs. Melt the butter in a pan and stir in the breadcrumbs. Remove from the heat immediately and allow to cool.

Skin the fish and cut into portions 6 ozs (170 g) approx. Season with salt and freshly ground pepper. Spread the leeks over the base of an ovenproof dish. Lay the pieces of fish on top of the leeks and coat with the Mornay sauce. Mix the remaining grated cheese with the buttered crumbs and sprinkle over the top. Pipe a ruff of fluffy Duchesse potato around the edge if you want to have a whole meal in one dish.

Cook in a moderate oven, 180°C/350°F/regulo 4, for 25–30 minutes or until the fish is cooked through and the top is golden brown and crisp. If necessary place under the grill for a minute or two before you serve to brown the edges of the potato.

Gratin of cod with buttered leeks may be served in individual dishes; scallop shells are particularly attractive, are completely ovenproof and may be used over and over again.

Variation

1. Omit the cheese and mustard from the sauce which will then be a Béchamel.
2. Streaky bacon cut into $\frac{1}{4}$ inch (5 mm) cubes and crisped is also good added to the leeks; use about $\frac{1}{4}$ lb (110 g).
3. Sauté mushrooms ($\frac{1}{2}$ lb/110 g/2 cups) and add to the leeks or instead of a layer of the leeks.
4. A layer of Piperonata (see *Simply Delicious 2*, page 61) or Tomato fondue (see *Simply Delicious 2*, page 67) under the fish is also very good.

Duchesse Potato

Serves 4

2 lbs (900 g) unpeeled potatoes, preferably Golden Wonders *or* Kerr's Pinks	1–2 egg yolks *or* 1 whole egg and 1 egg yolk
$\frac{1}{2}$ pint (300 ml/1$\frac{1}{4}$ cups) creamy milk	1–2 ozs (30–55 g/$\frac{1}{4}$–$\frac{1}{2}$ stick) butter

Scrub the potatoes well. Put them into a saucepan of cold water, add a good pinch of salt and bring to the boil. When the potatoes are about half cooked, 15 minutes approx. for 'old' potatoes, strain off two-thirds of the water, replace the lid on the saucepan, put on to a gentle heat and allow the potatoes to steam until they are cooked.

Peel immediately by just pulling off the skins, so you have as little waste as possible; mash while hot (see below). (If you have a large quantity, put the potatoes into the bowl of a food mixer and beat with the spade.)

While the potatoes are being peeled, bring about $\frac{1}{2}$ pint (300 ml) of milk to the boil. Beat the eggs into the hot mashed potatoes, and add enough boiling creamy milk to mix to a soft light consistency suitable for piping; then beat in the butter, the amount depending on how rich you like your potatoes. Taste and season with salt and freshly ground pepper.

Note: If the potatoes are not peeled and mashed while hot and if the boiling milk is not added immediately, the Duchesse potato will be lumpy and gluey.

If you only have egg whites they will be fine and will make a delicious light mashed potato also.

Fish Cakes with Garlic Butter

Makes 8

Fish cakes are absolutely scrummy when they are carefully made and served hot with a small blob of garlic butter melting on top.

½ lb (225 g/2 cups approx.) cold leftover fish, e.g. salmon, cod, haddock, hake (a proportion of smoked fish such as haddock or mackerel is good)
1 oz (30 g/¼ stick) butter
4 ozs (110 g/1 cup) onions, finely chopped
¼ lb (110 g/1 cup) mashed potato
1 egg yolk

1 tablesp. (1 American tablesp. + 1 teasp.) parsley, chopped
salt and freshly ground pepper
seasoned flour
1 beaten egg
fresh white breadcrumbs
clarified butter (see page 15) or a mixture of butter and oil for frying

Garlic butter
2 ozs (55 g/½ stick) butter
4 teasp. parsley, finely chopped

2–3 teasp. freshly squeezed lemon juice
2–3 cloves garlic, crushed

First make the garlic butter. Cream the butter, stir in the parsley and a few drops of lemon juice at a time. Add the crushed garlic. Roll into butter pats or form into a roll and wrap in greaseproof paper or tinfoil, screwing each end so that it looks like a cracker. Refrigerate to harden.

To make the fish cakes, melt the butter in a saucepan, toss in the chopped onion, cover and sweat on a gentle heat for 4 or 5 minutes until soft but not coloured.

Scrape the contents of the pan into a bowl, add the mashed potato and the flaked cooked fish, egg yolk and chopped parsley or a mixture of fresh herbs. Season well with salt and freshly ground pepper. Taste. Form the mixture into fish cakes about 2 ozs (55 g) each. Coat them first in seasoned flour, then in beaten egg and finally in crumbs. Refrigerate until needed, then cook on a medium heat in clarified butter until golden on both sides. Serve piping hot with pats or slices of garlic butter, Tomato fondue (see *Simply Delicious 2*, page 67) and a good green salad.

A Very Superior Fish Pie

Serves 6–8 approx. as a main course

1¼ lbs (675 g) fresh white fish
  e.g. hake, haddock, ling, cod,
  pollock *or* grey sea mullet
¼–½ lb (110–225 g) undyed
  smoked haddock *or* smoked
  mackerel *or* a proportion of
  smoked salmon trimmings
  could be used

¼ lb (110 g) cooked prawns *or*
  shrimps (see page 72)
1 lb (450 g) mussels—steam
  open, discard the shells and
  keep the juices (see page 89)

Béchamel sauce
3–4 slices of onion
3–4 slices of carrot
1 small bay leaf

a sprig of thyme
3 *or* 4 peppercorns
1 pint (600 ml/2½ cups) rich milk

3 hardboiled eggs
½ oz (15 g/1 American tablesp.)
  butter
1 clove garlic, crushed
5 ozs (140 g/1¼ cups) onions,
  chopped

6 ozs (170 g/3 cups) mushrooms,
  sliced
salt and freshly ground pepper
dash of cream (optional)

Roux
1 oz (30 g/¼ stick) butter

1 oz (30 g/scant ¼ cup) flour

1½ lbs (675 g/3 cups) Duchesse
  potato (see page 27)
1–2 tablesp. (1½–2½ American
  tablesp.) freshly grated
  Parmesan cheese

Put the onion, carrot, bay leaf, thyme and peppercorns into the milk, bring to the boil and simmer for 3–4 minutes, remove from the heat and leave to infuse for 10–15 minutes. Strain.

Meanwhile, hardboil the eggs for 10 minutes in boiling water, drain, cool and shell. Sauté the onion and garlic in the butter on a gentle heat for a few minutes, turn up the heat, add the sliced mushrooms, cook for a few minutes, season with salt and freshly ground pepper and set aside.

Cover the smoked fish in cold water and bring slowly to the boil. Discard the water.

Cut the fish fillets into 3–4 oz (85–110 g) pieces. Put the fresh and smoked fish into a wide pan or frying pan and cover with the flavoured milk. Season with salt and freshly ground pepper. Cover and simmer gently until the fish is cooked (5 minutes approx.). Take out the fish carefully and remove any bones or skin. Bring the liquid to the boil and thicken with roux. Add a little cream (optional) and the mussel juices, the chopped parsley, roughly chopped hardboiled egg, onion, mushrooms, pieces of fish and the prawns or shrimps and mussels. Stir very gently, taste and correct seasoning.

Spoon into one large or 6–8 small ovenproof dishes, pipe Duchesse potato on top and sprinkle with finely grated Parmesan cheese.* Put into a moderate oven, 180°C/350°F/regulo 4, to reheat and slightly crisp the potato on top (10–15 minutes approx. if the filling and potato are warm, or 30 minutes approx. if reheating the dish from cold). Serve with 'pats' or slices of garlic butter or Maître d'hôtel butter (see below).

*May be prepared ahead to this point.

Maître d'hôtel Butter
2 ozs (55 g/½ stick) butter   freshly squeezed juice of ½ lemon
4 teasp. parsley, finely chopped

Cream the butter, stir in the parsley and a few drops of lemon juice at a time. Roll into butter pats or form into a roll and wrap in greaseproof paper or tinfoil, screwing each end so that it looks like a cracker. Refrigerate to harden.

Omelette Arnold Bennett

Serves 1–2 as a main course

This delicious omelette would also be very good made with smoked salmon or smoked mackerel.

2–3 ozs (55–85 g) smoked
   haddock
a little milk
1 oz (30 g/¼ stick) butter
¼ pint (150 ml/generous ½ cup)
   cream

3 eggs
salt and freshly ground pepper
2–3 tablesp. (2–4 American
   tablesp.) Parmesan cheese,
   grated

Garnish
parsley, freshly chopped

10 inch (25.5 cm) omelette pan,
   preferably non-stick

Put the smoked haddock into a small saucepan. Cover with milk and simmer gently until it is cooked enough to separate into flakes (about 10 minutes). Drain. Toss the haddock over a moderate heat with half the butter and 2 tablespoons of the cream and keep aside. Separate the eggs, beat the yolks with a tablespoon of the cream and season with salt and freshly ground pepper. Whip the egg whites stiffly. Fold into the yolks with the haddock and add half the grated Parmesan cheese.

Melt the remaining butter in the omelette pan. Pour the mixture in gently and cook over a medium heat until the base of the omelette is golden. Spoon the remaining cream over the top and sprinkle with the rest of the finely grated Parmesan. Pop under a hot grill for a minute or so until golden and bubbly on top. Slide on to a hot dish, sprinkle with chopped parsley and serve immediately accompanied by a good green salad.

Ling or Pollock with Tomatoes and Fresh Spices

Serves 6 as a main course

Madhur Jaffrey has always been one of my favourite cookery writers. This recipe is based on a recipe from her book.

2¼ lbs (1.1 kg) ling *or* pollock fillets cut into 6 × 6 oz (170 g) pieces

¼ teasp. salt
½ teasp. cayenne pepper
¼ teasp. ground turmeric

Tomato sauce

4 tablesp. (5 American tablesp.) olive oil
1 teasp. fennel seeds
1 teasp. mustard seeds
6 ozs (170 g/1½ cups) onion, finely chopped
2 cloves garlic, peeled and crushed

2 teasp. ground cumin seeds
1 teasp. salt
¼ teasp. cayenne pepper
1 lb (450 g) very ripe tomatoes, peeled and chopped *or*
    1 × 14 oz (400 g) tin tomatoes
¼ teasp. garam masala (see below)

olive oil for frying

Mix the salt, cayenne pepper and turmeric together and sprinkle over both sides of the fish fillets. Cover and leave aside while you make the sauce.

Heat the olive oil in a saucepan. When it is hot, add the fennel and mustard seeds which will start to pop in a few seconds, then add the crushed garlic and chopped onions. Continue to cook until the onions turn golden, then add the ground cumin, salt and cayenne pepper. Stir and then add the tomatoes and juice, finally the garam masala. Bring to the boil and simmer gently for 15 minutes.

Preheat the oven to 180°C/350°F/regulo 4. Heat 2–3 tablespoons of olive oil in a frying pan, brown the pieces of fish on both sides and remove to a warm ovenproof serving dish. Cover with the tomato sauce and bake in the preheated oven for 13–15 minutes or until the fish is just cooked. Serve with new potatoes and a good green salad.

Madhur Jaffrey's Garam Masala

Makes about 3 tablesp. (4 American tablesp.)

Commercial garam masala loses its aromatic flavour very quickly, so it's best to make your own. Grind it in small quantities so that it is always fresh and used up quickly.

1 tablesp. (1 American tablesp. + 1 teasp.) green cardamom seeds	1 teasp. cumin seeds
	1 teasp. whole cloves
1 × 2-inch (5 cm) piece of cinnamon stick	1 teasp. black peppercorns
	¼ whole nutmeg

Put all the ingredients into a clean electric coffee grinder and whizz for about 30 seconds or until all the spices are finely ground. Store in a dark place in a tiny screwtop jar and use up quickly. Don't forget to clean out the coffee grinder really well or your coffee will certainly perk you up! Better still, if you use spices regularly, keep a grinder specially for that purpose.

Grey Sea Mullet

Best September–January

Here is my no. 1 nomination for the most under-appreciated fish in our waters. In my opinion a really fine grey *sea* mullet is every bit as good as sea bass at a fraction of the price. We have been enjoying it for years for a few pence a pound, but I have no doubt that very soon it will be 'discovered' and the price will soar, as was the case with monkfish. Take advantage of it while you can.

Grey sea mullet is a firm round fish, silvery grey in colour and with scales as large as a fingernail. With its strong mouth and formidable teeth, this fellow is considered by anglers to be quite a catch!

Grey Sea Mullet with Gruyère and Mustard

Serves 6 as a main course

This is one of the simplest and most delicious fish dishes I know — another gem which Jane Grigson taught us when she came to teach at the Ballymaloe Cookery School in 1989.

6 grey sea mullet fillets weighing 6 ozs (190 g) each (haddock, halibut, cod, brill, whiting *or* monkfish could be used instead)
$\frac{1}{4}$ oz (8 g/$\frac{1}{2}$ American tablesp.) butter
salt and freshly ground pepper

8 ozs (250 g/2 cups) grated Gruyère, Gouda *or* Emmental cheese
1 tablesp. (1 American tablesp. + 1 teasp.) Dijon mustard
4 tablesp. (5 American tablesp. approx.) cream

ovenproof dish $8\frac{1}{2}$ × 10 inches (21.5 × 25.5 cm)

Preheat the oven to 180°C/350°F/regulo 4. Lightly butter the ovenproof dish. Season the fish with salt and freshly ground pepper. Arrange the fillets in a single layer. Mix the grated cheese with the mustard and cream and spread carefully over the fish. Cook in the preheated oven for about 20 minutes or until the fish is cooked and the top is golden brown. Flash under the grill if necessary. Serve with new potatoes and a good green salad.

Deh Ta Hsiung's Chinese Steamed Whole Fish

Serves 4 as a main course

Deh Ta Hsiung, a Chinese chef who came to the school on several occasions to give us a 'Taste of China', was so excited by the flavour of grey sea mullet that he almost emigrated to Ireland! I give you his delicious recipe for steamed fish with his permission.

1 grey sea mullet *or* perch, 1½–2 lbs (680–900 g)	2 ozs (50 g) pork fillet *or* cooked ham, thinly shredded
1 teasp. salt	2 tablesp. light soy sauce
1 teasp. sesame seed oil	1 tablesp. rice wine *or* sherry
4 spring onions	2 slices peeled ginger root, thinly shredded
2–3 dried mushrooms, soaked and thinly shredded	2 tablesp. oil

Scale and gut the fish, wash it under the cold tap and dry it well both inside and out with a cloth or kitchen paper. Trim the fins and tail if not already trimmed, and slash both sides of the fish diagonally as far as the bone at intervals of about ½ inch (1 cm) with a sharp knife. (In case you wonder why it is necessary to slash both sides of the fish before cooking, the reason is twofold: first, if you cook the fish whole the skin will burst unless it is scored; and secondly it allows the heat to penetrate more quickly and at the same time helps to diffuse the flavours of the seasoning and sauce. Also, as the Chinese never use a knife at the table, it is much easier to serve the fish if you can pick up the pieces of flesh with just a pair of chopsticks.)

Rub about half the salt and all the sesame seed oil inside the fish, and place it on top of 2–3 spring onions on an oval-shaped dish.

Mix the mushrooms and pork with the remaining salt, a little of the soy sauce and the rice wine. Stuff about half of this mixture inside the fish and put the rest on top with the ginger root. Place in a hot steamer and steam vigorously for 15 minutes.

Meanwhile, thinly shred the remaining spring onions and heat the oil in a little saucepan until bubbling. Remove the fish dish from the steamer, arrange the spring onion shreds on top, pour the remaining soy sauce over it and then the hot oil from the head to tail. Serve hot.

If you don't possess a steamer big enough to hold a whole fish, it can be wrapped in silver foil and baked in the oven at 450°F/230°C/regulo 8 for 20–25 minutes.

Note: This recipe is taken from *The Home Book of Chinese Cookery* by Deh Ta Hsiung.

Salmon and Seatrout

Best March–August

My first taste of fresh salmon was at a wedding breakfast in Cahir, Co. Tipperary, when I was about eight, and my recollection of it is tinged with regret to this very day. I was discouraged from finishing my plateful in order to leave room for the next course—which sadly proved to be not half so delicious! Since I came to live in East Cork I have been spoiled summer after summer with what I consider to be the best salmon in the world, caught while it is still in the sea and charged with fat. And I'm not biased!

Wild Irish salmon is one of the greatest summer treats, something to be looked forward to like the first new potatoes, fresh green peas and asparagus that go so well with it. For goodness sake resist the temptation to fill your freezer with salmon—enjoy it as often as you can while it is in season and at its best, and then forget about it until the next year.

Wild Irish seatrout is much scarcer than salmon, but if you should be lucky enough to come across some, you can cook it very successfully using the fresh salmon recipes here.

Farmed salmon and seatrout are widely available all year round. They are generally considered to have a less fine flavour than the wild varieties but are reasonable value for money.

Salmon, 'the king of the sea', is a beautiful round fish with silvery scales and a slightly hooked mouth. Up to 8 lbs in weight it is termed a peel or grilse.

Seatrout, also known as salmon trout, looks very similar to a small salmon but is distinguishable by its back ventral fin which is white, whereas in a salmon it is streaked with black.

Roulade of Smoked Salmon with Cottage Cheese and Dill

Serves 4 as a starter

This very stylish smoked salmon recipe also makes delicious canapés served on thick cucumber slices.

4 slices of smoked salmon,
thinly sliced and about
6 inches (15 cm) long
4 ozs (110 g/$\frac{1}{2}$ cup) cream cheese
1 tablesp. (1 American tablesp.
+ 1 teasp.) finely chopped
chives *or* 1 dessertsp.
(2 American teasp.) finely
chopped dill

2 tablesp. (2 American tablesp.
+ 2 teasp.) cream
salt and freshly ground pepper
$\frac{1}{4}$ quantity cucumber salad (see
page 38)

Garnish
sprigs of fennel *or* chervil

Mix the cream cheese, chives or dill and cream together and season to taste with salt and freshly ground pepper. Spread the cheese mixture on to each slice of salmon and roll them up carefully. Cover and refrigerate for at least 1 hour.

Next make the cucumber salad (see page 38).

To assemble: Arrange 4 or 5 slices of cucumber salad on each plate. Cut the smoked salmon rolls into $\frac{1}{2}$–$\frac{3}{4}$ inch (1–2 cm) slices and place on top of the cucumber slices. Drizzle a little of the excess dressing from the cucumber salad on to the plate. Garnish with sprigs of fennel or chervil and serve immediately.

Warm Smoked Salmon with Cucumber and Dill

Serves 4 as a starter

Rory O'Connell serves this warm smoked salmon recipe on his special menu at Ballymaloe. We use Bill Casey's salmon which is smoked on our farm.

6–8 ozs (170–225 g) smoked Irish
salmon
$\frac{1}{4}$ oz (8 g/$\frac{1}{2}$ American tablesp.)
butter
6 tablesp. (8 American tablesp.)
cucumber, peeled and cut into
$\frac{1}{4}$ inch (5 mm) dice

salt, freshly ground pepper and
lemon juice
4 fl ozs (120 ml/$\frac{1}{2}$ cup) cream
2 teasp. chopped fennel *or*
1 teasp. chopped dill

Slice the smoked salmon straight down on to the skin into $\frac{1}{4}$ inch (5 mm) thick slices. Melt the butter in a sauté pan and allow to foam. Place the smoked salmon slices carefully in the pan, after 30 seconds

Seafood Chowder

Chinese Fish Soup with Spring Onions

Ballymaloe Hot Buttered Lobster

Lobster Mayonnaise

turn them carefully and add the cucumber dice. Season with salt, pepper and a squeeze of lemon juice. Add the cream and dill or fennel and allow the cream to bubble up and barely thicken. Check seasoning and serve immediately on hot plates.

Gravlax with Mustard and Dill Mayonnaise

Serves 12–16 as a starter

We are all addicted to this pickled salmon which keeps for up to a week. Fresh dill is essential.

$1\frac{1}{2}$–2 lbs (675–900g) tail piece of fresh wild Irish salmon

1 heaped tablesp. (2 American tablesp.) sea salt

1 heaped tablesp. (2 American tablesp.) sugar

1 teasp. freshly ground black pepper

2 tablesp. (2 American tablesp. + 2 teasp.) fresh dill, finely chopped

Fillet the salmon and remove all the bones with a tweezers. Mix the salt, sugar, pepper and dill together in a bowl. Place the fish on a piece of clingfilm and scatter the mixture over the surface of the fish. Wrap tightly with clingfilm and refrigerate for a minimum of 12 hours.

Mustard and dill mayonnaise

1 large egg yolk, preferably free range

2 tablesp. (2 American tablesp. + 2 teasp.) French mustard

1 tablesp. (1 American tablesp. + 1 teasp.) white sugar

$\frac{1}{4}$ pint (150 ml/generous $\frac{1}{2}$ cup) ground nut or sunflower

1 tablesp. (1 American tablesp. + 1 teasp.) white wine vinegar

1 tablesp. (1 American tablesp. + 1 teasp.) dill, finely chopped

salt and white pepper

Whisk the egg yolk with the mustard and sugar, drip in the oil drop by drop whisking all the time, then add the vinegar and fresh dill.

To serve, wipe the dill mixture off the salmon and slice thinly. Arrange on a plate in a rosette shape. Fill the centre of the rosette with mustard and dill mayonnaise. Garnish with fresh dill. Serve with brown bread and butter.

Salmon Tartare with a Sweet Cucumber Salad

Serves 6–8 as a starter

½ lb (225 g) wild Irish salmon, pickled as for Gravlax (see above)

1 teasp. homemade mayonnaise (see page 64)

squeeze of fresh lemon juice

tiny dash of sweet mustard

freshly ground pepper

¼ pint (150 ml/½ cup) sour cream, lightly whipped

Sweet cucumber salad

6 ozs (170 g/1 cup) approx. cucumber, thinly sliced

2 ozs (55 g/½ cup) approx. onion, thinly sliced

2 ozs (55 g/generous ¼ cup) sugar

1¼ level teasp. salt

1¼ fl ozs (35.5 ml/generous ⅛ cup) white wine vinegar

Garnish

small sprigs of dill

dill *or* **chive flowers**

Wash the Gravlax and dry well. Cut the salmon into tiny ⅛ inch (3 mm) dice and mix with the mayonnaise; add mustard and lemon juice. Season well with freshly ground pepper. Cover and leave in the fridge for 1 hour.

Meanwhile make the cucumber salad. Combine the sliced cucumber and onion in a large bowl. Mix sugar, salt and vinegar together and pour over the cucumber and onion. Place in a tightly covered container in the refrigerator and leave for at least 1 hour.

To serve the tartare, put a 2½ inch (6.5 cm) cutter on to each white plate, fill almost full with salmon mixture and smooth a little sour cream over the top with a palette knife. Lift off the cutter and put a ring of cucumber salad around the salmon tartare. Garnish the top with tiny sprigs of dill and perhaps some dill or chive flowers.

Serve with crusty white bread or hot toast.

Salmon with Tomato and Fresh Herb Salsa

Serves 6 as a main course

This is a refreshing new way of serving salmon with a distinct Californian flavour. This recipe would also be delicious for pan-grilled tuna fish steaks, a new arrival on the Irish market. Remember to cook them rare so they will be moist and juicy.

$2\frac{1}{4}$ lbs (1.1 kg) fresh wild Irish
   salmon

salt

Tomato and fresh herb salsa
6 very ripe tomatoes, peeled,
   seeded and cut into $\frac{1}{4}$ inch
   (5 mm) dice
1 tablesp. (1 American tablesp.
   + 1 teasp.) freshly chopped
   oregano (annual marjoram)
1 tablesp. (1 American tablesp.
   + 1 teasp.) basil

1 tablesp. (1 American tablesp.
   + 1 teasp.) parsley
1 tablesp. (1 American tablesp.
   + 1 teasp.) thyme leaves
4 fl ozs (120 ml/$\frac{1}{2}$ cup) Extra
   Virgin olive oil
1 teasp. sea salt
freshly ground pepper

First poach the salmon. Choose a saucepan which will barely fit the piece of fish: an oval cast iron one is usually perfect. Half fill with measured salted water (1 tablespoon salt to every 2 pints water), bring to the boil, put in the piece of fish, bring back to the boil, cover and simmer gently for 20 minutes. Turn off the heat, allow to sit in the water and serve within 15–20 minutes.

Mix together all the ingredients for the salsa, taste and correct seasoning. When the salmon is cooked divide into portions and serve on hot plates surrounded by the cold tomato and fresh herb salsa.

Note: The salmon may also be pan-grilled for this recipe.

Salmon with Lemon and Honey

Serves 6 as a main course

This combination doesn't sound very promising, but you'll be surprised how delicious it is, particularly if you can get some fresh horseradish.

$6 \times$ 4–6 oz (110–170 g) escalopes
   fresh wild salmon, $\frac{1}{2}$ inch
   (1 cm) thick approx.
sea salt and freshly ground
   pepper
$\frac{1}{2}$–1 oz (15–30 g/$\frac{1}{2}$–1 American
   tablesp.) butter

scant 2 tablesp. (2 American
   tablesp. + 2 teasp.) pure Irish
   honey
1–2 tablesp. ($1\frac{1}{2}$–$2\frac{1}{2}$ American
   tablesp.) freshly squeezed
   lemon juice
1 teasp. horseradish, freshly
   grated (optional)

Garnish
sprigs of fresh fennel, chervil *or*
   flat parsley

Season the salmon escalopes on both sides. Cook for 1 minute approx. on each side in a non-stick frying pan. Remove to a plate, immediately melt the butter in the pan with the honey and lemon juice, add the horseradish if using, allow to bubble for a second or two. Taste and correct the seasoning if necessary. Put the salmon back on to the pan and coat with the sauce. Transfer to a hot serving plate and serve immediately with the pan juices poured over the salmon.

Garnish with fresh fennel, chervil or flat parsley.

Trout

Brown best June
Farmed rainbow available all year round

Now that I live close to the sea, I have access mainly to seafish, but I still hanker after the flavour of the little brown trout that I got as a child from an old fisherman in Cullahill who used to produce them every so often as a special treat from the depths of his tweedy pockets.

Brown trout, which vary in size considerably, have silvery skin dappled with black or reddish spots, and may sometimes have a golden sheen. The flesh can be pink or white and somehow I always imagine that the pink ones taste better. Unfortunately river pollution has made brown trout much scarcer than before, but many angling clubs are doing their best to restock the rivers.

Rainbow trout have a more speckled skin and are easily recognisable by a broad iridescent band on each side of the body. As many fish shops have trout tanks they are often among the freshest fish available, but unfortunately do not have quite the same flavour as the wild species.

Unless you fish or have a good fishing friend, the trout you cook, whether brown or rainbow, will most probably have been farmed.

Trout with Ginger Butter

Serves 6 as a main course

This fresh ginger butter is also very good with other grilled fish such as salmon, sea bass or grey sea mullet.

6 fresh pink rainbow trout
salt and freshly ground pepper

olive oil for brushing

Ginger butter
3 ozs (85 g/¾ stick) unsalted butter
1 tablesp. (1 American tablesp. + 1 teasp.) finely chopped spring onion (scallion) *or* **shallot**

1½ tablesp. (2 American tablesp.) dry vermouth
1½ tablesp. (2 American tablesp.) fresh ginger, grated

Garnish
whole chives and chive flowers if available

41

First make the ginger butter. Melt $\frac{1}{2}$ oz (15 g) butter and sweat the spring onion or shallot for a few minutes over a gentle heat until it is almost soft, add the vermouth and cook until it has all been absorbed. Scrape this mixture into the bowl of a food processor and add the grated ginger. Whizz for a few seconds, allow to cool, add the remainder of the butter and whizz until smooth. Taste, season with salt and freshly ground pepper. Put into a bowl and refrigerate until needed.

Gut, fillet, wash and dry the trout carefully and season with salt and freshly ground pepper. Preheat a grillpan, brush the trout with olive oil and cook first flesh side down for 3 minutes approx., then turn over carefully and cook for a further 3 or 4 minutes on the skin side depending on the thickness of the fillets.

Serve on hot plates with a little ginger butter melting on top. Garnish with whole chives and chive flowers if available.

Trout with Mushrooms

Serves 4 as a main course

4 pink rainbow trout
seasoned flour (see glossary)
1 oz (30 g/$\frac{1}{4}$ stick) butter, clarified
  if possible (see page 15)
1 large clove garlic, crushed
1 shallot, finely chopped
8 oz (225 g/4 cups) mushrooms,
  sliced

2–3 tablesp. (2–4 American
  tablesp. approx.) Pernod
8 tablesp. (10 American tablesp.
  approx.) cream
2 teasp. parsley, chopped

Garnish
sprigs of parsley

Gut and fillet the trout and wash and dry the fillets carefully. Dip the trout in seasoned flour, melt half the butter and fry the fish in a wide frying pan, cooking in two batches if necessary. Keep warm.

Wipe out the pan. Melt the remaining butter on a low heat, cook the shallot for a few minutes, increase the heat and add the garlic and mushrooms. Season with salt and freshly ground pepper. When the mushrooms are cooked, add the Pernod to the pan and allow to boil for about 1 minute, then add the cream and parsley. Taste and if it is too thick add a little water. Spoon the sauce over the trout, garnish with sprigs of parsley and serve immediately.

Mackerel

Best July–September

It's no secret that I am particularly partial to fresh mackerel. I must have about forty recipes for this versatile fish which can be fried, poached, barbecued and even makes a wonderful soup. The most important thing to remember about mackerel is that it must be eaten absolutely fresh. Tommy Sliney to whose memory this book is dedicated always used to say that the sun should never set on a mackerel—in other words it should be eaten on the day it is caught, otherwise the flavour becomes rather bitter and the texture mushy. If you are on holiday by the sea, take advantage of it and feast yourself on mackerel for breakfast, dinner and tea!

Mackerel is an oily fish with a distinctive black zig-zag pattern on its silvery back, and a bluish sheen. Choose small to medium fish rather than large ones which can be dry and coarse.

*Barbecued or Pan-grilled Mackerel with Green Gooseberry Sauce

Serves 4 as a main course

I adore barbecued food, but I'm still struggling with the vagaries of this cooking medium. Somehow the coals are never quite at the right stage until you have finished cooking! However when you get it right everything tastes so delicious that it's worth persevering with. Salting fish before barbecuing enhances the flavour tremendously. I like to serve mackerel with the heads on, but if you are a bit squeamish remove them before cooking. Some garden shops sell fancy wire cages to barbecue fish in, which gets over the problem of the skin sticking to the grids. Alternatively, you could wrap the fish in tinfoil, which is also delicious.

4 very fresh mackerel   **olive oil**
sea salt

Gut, wash and dry the mackerel and cut about 3 slits on either side of the back with a sharp knife. About 15 minutes before cooking sprinkle the fish lightly with sea salt inside and outside. Just before cooking dry the fish thoroughly, brush lightly with olive oil and barbecue for 4–5 minutes on each side depending on the size. Serve with Green gooseberry sauce (see below).

Barbecued Mackerel in Tinfoil

Wash, dry and salt the mackerel as above, put a sprig of fennel in the centre and a knob of butter if you like. Wrap in tinfoil and seal the edges well. Put on the barbecue and cook for 4–6 minutes on each side depending on the size. Serve with a segment of lemon and let each person open their own package. There will be delicious juice to mop up with crusty bread or a baked potato.

Green Gooseberry Sauce

10 ozs (285 g/2 cups) fresh green
  gooseberries
stock syrup to cover (see
  below)—6 fl ozs (175 ml/$\frac{3}{4}$ cup)
  approx.

a knob of butter (optional)

Top and tail the gooseberries, put into a stainless steel saucepan, barely cover with stock syrup (see below), bring to the boil and simmer until the fruit bursts. Taste. Stir in a small knob of butter if you like but it is very good without it.

Stock Syrup

4 fl ozs (120 ml/$\frac{1}{2}$ cup) water
4 ozs (110 g/generous $\frac{1}{2}$ cup)
  sugar

Dissolve the sugar in the water and boil together for 2 minutes. Store in a covered jar in the refrigerator until needed. Stock syrup can also be used for sorbets, fruit salads or as a sweetener in homemade lemonade.

Poached Mackerel with Sauce de Quimper

Serves 4 as a main course, 8 as a starter

Warm poached mackerel served with this wonderful sauce is an absolute feast.

4 fresh mackerel
2 pints (1.1 L/5 cups) water

1 teasp. salt

Sauce de Quimper

2 eggs yolks, preferably free
   range
1 teasp. Dijon mustard
½ teasp. white wine vinegar

1 tablesp. (1 American tablesp.
   + 1 teasp.) parsley, chopped *or*
a mixture of chervil, chives,
   tarragon and fennel, chopped
2 ozs (55 g/½ stick) butter, melted

Cut the heads off the mackerel, gut and clean them but keep whole. Bring the water to the boil, add the salt and the mackerel. Bring back to boiling point, cover and remove from the heat. After about 5–8 minutes, check to see whether the fish are cooked. The flesh should lift off the bone.

Meanwhile make the sauce. Put the egg yolks in a bowl, add the mustard, wine vinegar and the herbs, mix well and then whisk in the hot melted butter little by little so that the sauce emulsifies. When the mackerel is cool enough to handle remove to a plate, skin and lift the flesh carefully from the bones. Arrange on a serving dish, coat with the sauce and serve while still warm with a good green salad.

Mackerel with Cream and Dill

Serves 4 as a main course, 8 as a starter

Dill, which is an annual herb, is particularly good with mackerel. One wouldn't normally think of cream with an oily fish but this combination is surprisingly delicious and very fast to cook.

4 fresh mackerel
salt and freshly ground pepper
¼ oz (8 g/½ American tablesp.)
   butter

6 fl ozs (175 ml/¾ cup) cream
1½–2 tablesp. (2–2½ American
   tablesp.) fresh dill, finely
   chopped

Gut the mackerel, fillet carefully, wash and dry well. Season with salt and freshly ground pepper. Melt the butter in a frying pan, fry the mackerel fillets flesh down until golden brown, turn over on to the skin side, add cream and freshly chopped dill. Simmer gently for 3 or 4 minutes or until the mackerel is cooked, taste the sauce and serve immediately.

Deepfried Mackerel with Tartare Sauce

Serves 4 as a main course, 8 as a starter

Every summer the arrival of the mackerel into Ballycotton is eagerly awaited — usually around late July and early August. When the shoals are in, virtually anyone could dangle a line over the end of the pier and ·

catch a mackerel. I once did but when I caught a fish I was so upset I never tried again!

4 fresh mackerel
white flour seasoned with salt
 and freshly ground pepper
2 eggs, whisked with a little
 milk

fresh white breadcrumbs
olive *or* sunflower oil for deep
 frying

Tartare sauce

Serves 8–10

2 hardboiled egg yolks
2 raw egg yolks, preferably free
 range
¼ teasp. Dijon mustard
1–2 tablesp. (2 American tablesp.
 approx.) white wine vinegar
12 fl ozs (350 ml/1½ cups)
 sunflower *or* arachide oil *or*
 10 fl ozs (300 ml/1¼ cups) of
 either plus 2 fl ozs (50 ml/
 ¼ cup) olive oil

salt and freshly ground pepper
1 teasp. chopped capers
1 teasp. chopped gherkins
2 teasp. chopped chives *or* 2
 teasp. chopped spring onions
 (scallions)
2 teasp. chopped parsley
2 teasp. finely diced cucumber
 flesh (optional)
chopped white of the 2
 hardboiled eggs

Garnish
lemon segments

sprigs of parsley

First make the tartare sauce. Sieve the hardboiled egg yolks into a bowl, add the raw egg yolks, mustard and 1 tablespoon of wine vinegar. Mix well and whisk in the oil drop by drop, increasing the volume as the mixture thickens. When all the oil has been absorbed, add the other ingredients—capers, gherkins, chives or spring onions, parsley and cucumber dice. Then roughly chop the hardboiled egg white and fold in gently, taste, season and add a little more vinegar or a squeeze of fresh lemon juice if necessary.

Note: A quick tartare sauce can be made by adding the extra ingredients to a homemade mayonnaise but it is not quite the same.

To prepare the fish, gut and wash the mackerel, fillet carefully and dry in kitchen paper. Preheat the deep fryer to 180°C/350°F. Coat each piece first in seasoned flour, then in egg and finally in crumbs. When the oil is hot enough, fry a few fillets at a time and drain on kitchen paper. Serve on hot plates with a segment of lemon and a sprig of fresh parsley or deepfried parsley and tartare sauce. A Gigas oyster shell makes a pretty container for the sauce on each plate.

Herring

Best November–March

I get a 'woops' in my tummy every time the first basket of herrings comes in around November. I can never quite rationalise why this fish, which is cheaper than any other, gets me so excited, but for days after the season starts I prepare herrings in every possible way—fresh, salted or pickled. I also take some up to my German neighbours who smoke them to perfection to produce proper breakfast kippers.

Herrings are shimmering silver fish, darker on top. They are oily and quite bony, which seems to prejudice some people against them, but once you are familiar with the bone structure the source of the trouble can be easily removed.

Soused Herring or Mackerel

Serves 8 as a main course, 16 as a starter

Somehow it always seems to be a feast or a famine with herring or mackerel. If you have more than you can eat immediately this recipe could be the answer.

8 herrings *or* mackerel	1 teasp. sugar
1 thinly sliced onion	1 bay leaf
1 teasp. whole black peppercorns	$\frac{1}{2}$ pint (300 ml/$1\frac{1}{4}$ cups) white
6 whole cloves	wine vinegar
1 teasp. salt	

Gut, wash and fillet the herrings or mackerel, making sure there are no bones. Roll up the fillets skin side out and pack tightly into a cast iron casserole. Sprinkle over thinly sliced onion, peppercorns, cloves, salt, sugar, vinegar and a bay leaf. Bring to the boil on top of the cooker. Put into a very low oven, 140°C/275°F/regulo 1, and cook for 30–45 minutes.

Allow to get quite cold. Soused herring or mackerel will keep for 7–10 days in the fridge.

Soused Herring or Mackerel Salad with Dill Mayonnaise

Serves 4 as a main course, 8 as a starter

8 soused herrings *or* mackerel	cucumber salad (see page 65)
piped potato salad (see page 66)	green salad
tomato salad (see page 66)	Dill mayonnaise (see page 37)

Allow each person 1–2 soused herrings or mackerel, a portion of piped potato salad, tomato salad, cucumber salad and a little tossed green salad. Serve with Dill mayonnaise.

Herrings Grilled with Mustard Butter

Serves 6 as a main course

6 fresh herrings, gutted, scaled and washed	olive oil
	sea salt

Mustard butter

2 teasp. Dijon mustard	3 ozs (85 g/$\frac{3}{4}$ stick) melted butter
1 tablesp. (1 American tablesp. + 1 teasp.) parsley, finely chopped	squeeze of fresh lemon juice

Slash the herrings in 2 or 3 places on each side. Coat with olive oil and sprinkle with salt. Heat a cast iron grill pan until hot and cook the herrings for approx. 6 minutes or until golden on both sides.

Meanwhile make the sauce. Put the mustard into a bowl, add the chopped parsley, gradually whisk in the hot melted butter and add a squeeze of lemon juice. Serve with the hot herrings.

Alternatively cream the butter with the mustard, add the finely chopped parsley, a good squeeze of fresh lemon juice and freshly ground pepper. Form into a roll and allow to harden or make into pats. Serve with the hot herrings.

Proper Breakfast Kippers

Serves 2

Our neighbour Mrs Schwartau smokes the very best kippers I have ever tasted. I like them best cooked for breakfast by what I call the jug method.

2 undyed kippers
Maître d'hôtel butter (see page 30)

Garnish
2 segments of lemon   **2 sprigs of parsley**

Put the kippers head downwards into a deep jug. Cover them with boiling water right up to their tails as though you were making tea. Leave for 5–10 minutes to heat through. Lift them out carefully by the tail and serve immediately on hot plates with a pat of Maître d'hôtel butter (see page 30) melting on top. Garnish each with a segment of lemon and a sprig of parsley.

Monkfish

Best March–October

For years the status of monkfish was so lowly that it had no identity of its own, and usually masqueraded as lobster or prawns. Then suddenly its firm, almost meaty flesh became fashionable and the price soared. Even so, monkfish is still well worth the money, particularly as it holds its shape so well no matter how you cook it, and with just one central bone there is almost no waste.

Monkfish is also called angler because of the two dorsal fins which look like fishing rods. It is easy to recognise because it has the most extraordinarily ugly face. Mercifully this is not normally on view in the fishmonger's—it would be almost enough to put you off your dinner! Here only the tail is used but in France the cheek pieces are considered a great delicacy.

Poached Monkfish with Red Pepper Sauce

Serves 6 as a main course

This is by far the most popular monkfish dish in our restaurant. Serve it sparingly for a special occasion and don't compromise the recipe!

$1\frac{1}{2}$ lbs (675 g) monkfish tails, carefully trimmed of skin and membrane

2 pints (1.1 L/5 cups) water
1 dessertsp. (2 American teasp.) salt

Sauce
1 red pepper
5 ozs (140 g/$1\frac{1}{4}$ stick) butter

8 fl ozs (250 ml/1 cup) cream

Garnish
sprigs of flat parsley *or* chervil

Cut the monkfish tails into $\frac{1}{2}$ inch (1 cm) collops (see glossary) and refrigerate until needed. Seed the red pepper and dice the flesh into $\frac{1}{8}$ inch (3 mm) cubes. Sweat gently in 1 teaspoonful of butter in a covered pot until soft (it's really easy to burn this so turn off the heat after a few minutes and it will continue to cook in the pot).

Put the cream into a saucepan and gently reduce to about 3 table-spoons or until it is in danger of burning, then whisk in the butter bit by bit as though you were making a Hollandaise sauce. Finally stir in the diced red pepper. Thin with warm water if necessary and keep warm.

Bring the water to the boil and add the salt. Add the collops of monkfish and simmer for 4-5 minutes or until completely white and no longer opaque. Drain well. Arrange in a warm serving dish or on individual plates, coat with the red pepper sauce, garnish with sprigs of flat parsley or chervil and serve immediately.

Monkfish with Red Pepper Vinaigrette

Serves 4-6 as a starter

Despite the name, this recipe is completely different from the previous one. No butter or cream this time!

12 ozs (340 g) monkfish fillet cut into $\frac{1}{2}$ inch (1 cm) collops (see glossary)

$\frac{1}{2}$ red pepper cut into $\frac{1}{8}$ inch (3 mm) dice or diamonds

Vinaigrette
4 tablesp. (5 American tablesp. + 1 teasp.) Extra Virgin olive oil
2 tablesp. (2 American tablesp. + 2 teasp.) sunflower oil

2 tablesp. (2 American tablesp. + 2 teasp.) sherry *or* balsamic vinegar (see glossary)
salt, freshly ground pepper and sugar to taste

Garnish
1 dessertsp. (2 American teasp.) chives, finely chopped

Put the dice of pepper flesh and the ingredients for the vinaigrette into a bowl and mix well together. Taste it carefully for seasoning. Keep the dressing in a warm place.

Steam or poach the monkfish in boiling salted water until just cooked (1 teasp. salt to 2 pints/1.1 L water). Watch it carefully—it will take about 4-5 minutes. The fish should look white and no longer opaque.

Drain the fish on kitchen paper and place on hot plates. Spoon the vinaigrette over and sprinkle with the chopped chives. Serve immediately.

*Monkfish Spedino with Summer Marjoram Sauce

Serves 4

There are lots of variations you can do on the kebab theme. This Italian spedino recipe is quick, easy and irresistible. Use unsmoked bacon and leave out the peppercorns or vary the herbs if you like.

1 lb (450 g) monkfish, cut into 1 inch (2.5 cm) cubes
4–6 smoked streaky bacon rashers, cut into 1 inch (2.5 cm) squares
1 small red pepper, cut into 1 inch (2.5 cm) squares
bulbs of tiny spring onions (scallions)—optional

1 level teasp. whole black peppercorns
1 level teasp. sea salt
2 tablesp. (2 American tablesp. + 2 teasp.) fennel (herb), freshly chopped
olive oil

Garnish
segments of lemon

Summer marjoram sauce

2 heaped tablesp. (3 American tablesp. + 1 teasp.) annual marjoram leaves (no stalk)
1 scant level teasp. sea salt
1 teasp. sugar

1 tablesp. (1 American tablesp. + 1 teasp.) lemon juice
4–6 tablesp. (5–7 American tablesp.) Extra Virgin olive oil

First make the sauce. Pound the marjoram with the sea salt and sugar in a pestle and mortar until completely crushed. Slowly add the lemon juice and olive oil as for mayonnaise.

Thread the monkfish, bacon, pepper and spring onion (if used) alternately on the skewers. Crack the black peppercorns in a pestle and mortar, add the sea salt and freshly chopped fennel. Spread this mixture out on to a work top or plate. Roll the spedino in it, then cover and refrigerate until the barbecue or chargrill is hot enough for cooking. Brush with a little olive oil—they usually take about 4–5 minutes on each side. Serve drizzled with Summer marjoram sauce or Beurre blanc (see page 81).

Note: The spedino can be cooked under a radiant grill also.

Ray or Skate

Best March–October

This is another contender for the title of Most Underestimated Fish in the Sea. Sadly it has very much a 'poor relation' image, partly because some people just associate it with ray and chips. In my opinion ray is a wonderful fish with succulent strands of flesh which can easily be lifted off the central layer of ribbed bone. It is one of the few fish which actually improves with keeping, losing the toughness it has when freshly caught—but a day or two is enough! Some people are put off by its slimy appearance and the daunting prospect of skinning it, but I've always cooked it with the skin on and find it very easy to remove it later. Children also love ray—lift the sweet flesh off the bones for them.

Ray (also known as skate) is large and kite-shaped with a long tail. The wedges sold by fishmongers come from the wings only.

Skate with Black Butter

Serves 2 as a main course

This classic recipe is one of the most delicious ways of serving a piece of really fresh skate wing.

1 medium skate (ray) wing
  weighing 1¼–1½ lbs (560–675 g)
1 onion, sliced
2 tablesp. (2 American tablesp.
  + 2 teasp.) white wine vinegar

a few sprigs of parsley
a little salt

Black butter
2 ozs (55 g/¼ stick) butter
2 tablesp. (2 American tablesp.
  + 2 teasp.) white wine vinegar

Garnish
parsley, chopped

Choose a pan wide enough for the skate to lie flat while cooking. Put the skate in, cover completely with cold water, add the onion, parsley, salt and 2 tablespoons of wine vinegar. Bring to the boil gently, cover and barely simmer for 15–20 minutes. If the flesh lifts easily from the cartilage the skate is cooked. Turn off the heat and transfer the fish on to a large serving plate. Skin and lift the flesh on to hot plates, first from one side of the cartilage, then the other, scraping off the white skin. Cover and keep hot.

Next make the black butter. Melt the butter immediately on a hot pan, allow it to foam and just as it turns brown add the wine vinegar, allow to bubble up again and then pour sizzling over the fish. Sprinkle with chopped parsley and serve immediately.

*Warm Ray Wing with Coriander

Serves 4 as a starter, 2 as a main course

The French are very fond of serving warm fish with a cold dressing. The coriander makes this dressing particularly delicious.

1 medium ray wing	2 tablesp. (2 American tablesp.
1 onion	+ 2 teasp.) white wine vinegar
2–3 sprigs of parsley	pinch of salt

Dressing

4 tablesp. (5 American tablesp. + 1 teasp.) olive oil	salt and freshly ground pepper
2 tablesp. (2 American tablesp. + 2 teasp.) sunflower *or* arachide oil	$\frac{1}{2}$ teasp. Dijon mustard
	1 teasp. coriander seeds
2 tablesp. (2 American tablesp. + 2 teasp.) sherry vinegar *or* balsamic vinegar	1 tablesp. (1 American tablesp. + 1 teasp.) green spring onion (scallion) cut at an angle

Poach the ray wing (see Skate with black butter for method). Lift the flesh off the bone and divide it into 2 or 4 portions.

Meanwhile make the dressing by combining the oils, sherry vinegar, salt, freshly ground pepper and mustard. Warm the coriander seed for a few minutes, crush in a pestle and mortar and add to the dressing. Just before serving add the spring onion tops and spoon over the warm ray wing.

Serve immediately on warm plates. This dish is best eaten lukewarm.

*Poached Ray Wing with Cucumber Hollandaise

Serves 4 as a starter, 2 as a main course

Simply Exquisite!

1 medium ray wing
1 onion, sliced
2–3 sprigs of parsley

2 tablesp. (2 American tablesp.
+ 2 teasp.) white wine vinegar
pinch of salt

Cucumber Hollandaise
2 egg yolks
4 ozs (110 g/1 stick) butter, diced
1 dessertsp. (2 teasp.) cold water
1 teasp. approx. lemon juice

¼ cucumber, peeled and cut into
tiny dice ⅛ inch (3 mm) approx.
¼ oz (8 g/½ American tablesp.)
butter
salt and freshly ground pepper

Garnish
sprigs of fennel

Poach the ray wing (see Skate with black butter for method).

Meanwhile make the Hollandaise sauce. Put the egg yolks into a heavy bottomed stainless steel saucepan on a very low heat, or in a bowl over hot water. Add cold water and whisk thoroughly. Add the butter bit by bit, whisking all the time. As soon as one piece melts, add the next. The mixture will gradually thicken, but if it shows signs of becoming too thick or 'scrambling' slightly remove from the heat immediately and add a little cold water if necessary. Do not leave the pan or stop whisking until the sauce is made. Finally add the lemon juice to taste. If the sauce is slow to thicken it may be because you are excessively cautious and the heat is too low. Increase the heat slightly and continue to whisk until the sauce thickens to coating consistency. Pour into a bowl and keep warm over hot but not boiling water. Melt ¼ oz (8 g/½ American tablesp.) butter and toss the cucumber in it for 1–2 minutes. Add to the Hollandaise sauce.

When the fish is cooked, remove the skin and lift the flesh from the bone as in the previous recipe. Put the fish on to hot plates and spoon over the Cucumber Hollandaise. Garnish with sprigs of fresh fennel and serve immediately.

Note: A quick Hollandaise can be made by whisking boiling butter into the egg yolks, drop by drop initially and then in a steady stream as for mayonnaise. Sharpen with a few drops of lemon juice at the end.

Ray and Mushroom Tart

Serves 6 as a main course

This is an absolutely delicious tart inspired by a recipe in Jane Grigson's *Fish Cookery*. Skate or ray wing cooked this way could be served as a filling for vol au vents or surrounded by a border of potato in scallop shells, or simply as a fish pie with a top of potato or overlapping croûtons.

1 medium ray wing
1 onion, sliced
2–3 sprigs of parsley
2 tablesp. (2 American tablesp. + 2 teasp.) white wine vinegar
pinch of salt
3 ozs (85 g/1½ cups) mushrooms, chopped

½ clove garlic, crushed
1 oz (30 g/¼ stick) butter
½ tin anchovy fillets, chopped
2½ fl ozs (70 ml/generous ¼ cup) double cream
salt and freshly ground pepper
chopped parsley

Shortcrust pastry
4 ozs (110 g/generous ¾ cup) flour
pinch of salt
2–3 ozs (55–85 g/½–¾ stick) butter

1 egg yolk
2 teasp. cold water

Béchamel sauce
1 oz (30 g/¼ stick) butter
1 tablesp. (1 American tablesp. + 1 teasp.) flour

½ pint (300 ml/1¼ cups) milk
salt and freshly ground pepper

Topping
1 tablesp. (1 American tablesp. + 1 teasp.) Gruyère cheese, grated

1 tablesp. (1 American tablesp. + 1 teasp.) buttered crumbs (see page 25)

7 inch (18 cm) flan ring

First make the pastry. Sieve the flour with the salt and rub in the butter. Beat the egg yolk with the cold water and bind the mixture with this. You may need a little more water, but do not make the pastry too wet—it should come away cleanly from the bowl. Wrap in clingfilm and rest for 15–30 minutes. Roll out thinly on a floured board and use it to line the flan ring. Line with greaseproof paper, fill with dried beans and bake blind in a preheated moderate oven, 180°C/350°F/regulo 4, for about 20–25 minutes or until almost cooked. Remove the beans and paper and allow to cool.

Take a pan sufficiently wide for the ray wing to lie flat while cooking. Cover it completely with cold water, add onion, parsley, salt and wine vinegar. Bring gently to the boil, cover and let barely simmer for 15–20 minutes or until the flesh will lift off the bone completely. Lift the ray wing out on to a plate with a slotted spoon. Remove the skin, lift the flesh off the bone and cut it into 1 inch (2.5 cm) pieces.

Meanwhile melt the butter for the béchamel, stir in the flour and gradually add the hot milk, beating well between additions. Leave to cook very slowly for 20 minutes, stirring now and then until you have a thick, creamy sauce (use a heat diffuser mat if you have one).

Sauté the mushrooms and garlic in the butter for 5 minutes. Add the anchovies, stir well and add the cream. Reduce to a fairly thick sauce. Add to the béchamel and leave to simmer over a low heat for a couple of minutes. Season and add the parsley.

Put a thin layer of sauce into the pastry case, arrange the fish on top, then spoon enough sauce over to cover it well. Sprinkle the top with the Gruyère cheese mixed with the buttered crumbs. Reheat in a fairly hot oven, 200°C/400°F/regulo 6, for 10–15 minutes approx. Serve with a green salad.

John Dory

Best March–October

Here is another handsome chap whose appearance has deterred a great many people from buying and savouring him! Again my advice is to try John Dory if you come across it, because the flavour is quite superb—comparable with turbot or sole—and the price not at all exorbitant.

John Dory is a fierce-looking yellowish-brown flat fish. Many cultures consider it to be a sacred fish, and because of the distinct thumb prints of St Peter on both sides, it is actually called St Peter's fish in several languages.

Grilled John Dory with Orange Butter

Serves 4

4 fillets John Dory, scaled
seasoned flour (see glossary)

a little butter

Orange butter
1 orange
2 ozs (55 g/½ stick) butter

¼ teasp. Hungarian paprika
sea salt

Garnish
segments of orange

chervil *or* flat parsley

Make the orange butter first. Grate the rind from the orange on the finest part of a stainless steel grater. Cut the orange in half and squeeze out the juice. Cream the butter, add the orange rind and paprika and gradually incorporate the orange juice, season with sea salt and make into a roll. Wrap in greaseproof paper and keep in the fridge until needed.

Dip the fish fillets in seasoned flour and smear a little butter on the flesh side. Heat a cast iron grill pan and cook the fish on a medium heat until golden on each side. Serve on hot plates with a slice of orange butter on each fillet and garnish with a segment of orange and some chervil or flat parsley.

Squid

Best September–December

Even adventurous cooks often have to take a deep breath when they are dealing with squid. Its physical characteristics—those curling tentacles and the ink sac that bursts all over your worktop—can be downright offputting. To make matters worse the word has got around that squid is tough and chewy, full stop, so many people decide that it's not worth bothering about.

I have discovered the great secret is to cook it either for a very short time (from 30 seconds to 2–3 minutes) or for a very long time (1–1½ hours). For some extraordinary reason the toughness creeps in somewhere in the intervening period and it then absolutely deserves its rubbery reputation.

Squid looks rather like a baby octopus. Its body is translucent white with pinkish tentacles. It can be cooked in many different ways, including in its own ink, and the sac makes a perfect receptacle for stuffing. Trendy chefs in California buy squid ink at enormous expense to colour their black designer pasta. Whatever turns you on!

*Squid Provençal

Serves 4 as a main course, 8 as a starter

Remember squid only takes a couple of minutes to cook. This way it will taste sweet and tender and convert even the most ardent squid hater!

4 medium-sized squid
4–5 tablesp. (5–6 American tablesp.) olive oil
2 large onions, sliced
2 cloves garlic, crushed
6 fl ozs (175 ml/¾ cup) dry white wine

5 large tomatoes, peeled, seeded and sliced
½ teasp. Hungarian paprika
salt, freshly ground pepper and sugar
1 tablesp. (1 American tablesp. + 1 teasp.) parsley, chopped

To prepare the squid, cut off the tentacles just in front of the eyes and remove the beak. Pull the entrails out of the sac and discard. Catch the tip of the quill and pull it out of the sac. (Now you know why the squid is called the scribe of the sea.) Pull off the wings and scrape the purplish membrane off them and the sac. Wash the sac, wings and tentacles well.

Heat the olive oil in a wide saucepan, toss in the crushed garlic and sliced onions, cover and sweat for 5 minutes on a gentle heat. Add the .wine and reduce.

Meanwhile, peel and slice the tomatoes and add to the onions with the paprika. Season with salt, pepper and sugar and cook uncovered until thickish (about 10 minutes).*

Just before serving add the squid and chopped parsley, cover the saucepan and cook for 2–3 minutes or until the colour changes. Taste, correct seasoning and serve immediately.

*May be prepared ahead to this point.

*Squid with Garlic Butter

Serves 4 as a starter, 2 as a main course

2 medium-sized squid
2 tablesp. (2 American tablesp.
+ 2 teasp.) approx. garlic
butter (see page 28)

Garnish
segments of lemon

First prepare the squid (see recipe above). Cut the sac into $\frac{1}{4}$ inch (5 mm) rings, the tentacles into 2 inch (5 cm) strips and the wings into $\frac{1}{4}$ inch (5 mm) strips across the grain.

Just before serving, heat 4 plates. Melt about 1 tablespoon of garlic butter in the frying pan, allow to foam, toss in the squid (do it in two batches if necessary). Toss around for 30-60 seconds or until the pieces turn from opaque to white. Serve instantly on hot plates with a segment of lemon on each.

Stuffed Squid with Tomato Sauce

Serves 6 as a main course

Squid sacs make the perfect receptacle for stuffing. They plump up like little white cushions and are delicious with tomato sauce.

6 medium squid—bodies
6–8 inches (15–20.5 cm) long

Stuffing

4 tablesp. (5 American tablesp.
+ 1 teasp.) Extra Virgin olive
oil
2 ozs (55 g/$\frac{1}{3}$ cup) smoked streaky
bacon, rind removed, cut into
$\frac{1}{8}$ inch (3 mm) dice
1 lb (450 g/4 cups) onions,
chopped
2 cloves garlic, crushed
1$\frac{1}{2}$ ozs (45 g/$\frac{1}{2}$ cup) mushrooms,
finely chopped

1$\frac{1}{2}$ ozs (45 g/$\frac{3}{4}$ cup) white
breadcrumbs
1 tablesp. (1 American tablesp.
+ 1 teasp.) parsley, chopped
1 tablesp. (1 American tablesp.
+ 1 teasp.) fresh oregano
(annual marjoram)
salt and freshly ground pepper

Tomato sauce

2 tablesp. (2 American tablesp.
+ 2 teasp.) olive oil
2 cloves garlic, sliced
1 × 14 oz (400 g) tin tomatoes,
chopped

salt, freshly ground pepper and
sugar
3 leaves of fresh basil

Garnish
flat parsley, chopped

Prepare the squid in the usual way (see recipe for Squid Provençal, page 59). Wash the sacs well and leave whole. Chop the wings and tentacles into $\frac{1}{4}$ inch (5 mm) pieces.

Next make the stuffing. Heat the olive oil in a saucepan, add the bacon and cook for a few minutes until crisp and golden. Add the onion and crushed garlic, cover and sweat for 5 or 6 minutes on a gentle heat.

Next make the tomato sauce. Toss the sliced garlic in the olive oil in a wide saucepan for 1–2 minutes, add the chopped tomatoes and their juice. Season with salt, freshly ground pepper and a pinch of sugar. Cook for about 5 minutes and add the torn basil.

Turn up the heat under the onion and bacon, add the mushrooms and tentacles and toss around for a few minutes. Add the breadcrumbs, chopped parsley and oregano and season with salt and freshly ground pepper. Taste. Carefully fill the squid sacs with stuffing—no more than two-thirds full or else they may burst. Secure the openings with cocktail sticks.

Lay the stuffed squid in a single layer on top of the tomato sauce, turn them in the sauce, cover with a paper lid and the lid of the saucepan. Cook on the very lowest heat for 30–40 minutes or put into a preheated oven, 180°/350°F/regulo 4, if you want to get it out of the way. Serve surrounded with sauce and sprinkled with chopped parsley.

Note: If the squid are very large they can take up to 1 hour to cook. If you would like more sauce just double the quantity of sauce ingredients.

*Chargrilled Squid with Fresh Chilli Sauce

Serves 8 as a starter

3–4 medium-sized squid

Fresh chilli sauce
3 cloves garlic
8 tablesp. (1 cup) flat leaf Italian parsley, finely chopped
1 large red chilli, seeded and finely chopped

4 fl ozs (scant 150 ml/½ cup) Extra Virgin olive oil
sea salt and freshly ground black pepper
olive oil for grilling

To serve
rocket leaves

Extra Virgin olive oil

Prepare the squid as described on page 59. Cut the sac and wings into pieces approx. 2 inches (5 cm) square and lightly score the inside of each piece with the tip of a knife. Separate the tentacles. Cover and refrigerate until needed.

To make the sauce, chop the garlic with the seeded and chopped chilli, (use a mezzaluna if you have one), add the parsley and continue to chop until fine. Put into a bowl with the olive oil and season with salt and freshly ground pepper. (This sauce will keep a week in the fridge and is also good served with prawns or steak!)

Just before serving heat the chargrill or a cast iron grill pan. Toss the rocket leaves in a little olive oil. Brush the squid pieces with olive oil and put them on the very hot chargrill for a few seconds on each side—just long enough for them to change colour and be marked by the grill. Lay on a bed of rocket leaves, spoon a little chilli sauce over each piece of squid and serve immediately.

Lobster

Best May–September

To me, Irish lobster is one of the very best things to eat in the whole wide world. The sad thing is that for many people, an eagerly anticipated feast can turn out to be an expensive disappointment. The trouble is that lobsters are sometimes stored in tanks for weeks on end, and that naturally impairs their flavour. Lobster is at its very best straight from the sea. Even if I was never to taste a bit of lobster again, I wouldn't dream of buying frozen, imported, cooked lobster. It's a travesty, compared to the exquisite Irish lobster, and a total waste of money.

Live lobsters are navy blue and only turn orange when cooked — a fact which comes as a surprise to many people. Classified as a crustacean, the lobster has two large pincers which the fisherman will normally have secured with rubber bands — a necessary precaution because it's no exaggeration to say that they can break your finger. Size varies; the optimum, usually snapped up by restaurants, is $1\frac{1}{2}$–2 lbs. The flesh of bigger lobsters is slightly coarser but still wonderful served in a delicious sauce. Please, please *do not* buy lobsters below the approved minimum size, which will weigh approximately $\frac{3}{4}$lb. If we eat all the young stock, our grandchildren will be denied this extra special treat.

How to Cook Lobster or Crayfish

Serves 2–4

The method described here is considered by the RSPCA to be the most humane way to cook lobster and certainly results in deliciously tender and juicy flesh. When we are cooking lobster we judge by colour, but if you are uneasy about that allow 15 minutes for the first lb (450 g) and 10 minutes per lb after that.

2 × 2 lb (900g) live lobsters

Court bouillon
1 carrot
1 onion
1 pint (600 ml/2$\frac{1}{2}$ cups) water
1 pint (600 ml/2$\frac{1}{2}$ cups) dry white wine

bouquet garni: parsley stalks, sprig of thyme, celery stalks and a small bay leaf
6 peppercorns
no **salt**

Cover the lobsters or crayfish with lukewarm salted water (6 ozs/170 g/ $\frac{7}{8}$ cup salt to every 4 pints/2.3 L/10 cups water). Put the saucepan on a low heat and bring slowly to simmering point: lobster and crab die at about 44°C/112°F. By this stage the lobsters will be changing colour so remove them and discard all the cooking water.

Slice the carrot and onion and put with the wine, fresh water, herbs and peppercorns into a stainless steel saucepan and bring to the boil, replace the lobsters and cover with a tight-fitting lid. Steam them until they change colour to bright red, and remove them from the pot. Strain the cooking liquid and reserve for a sauce.

*Lobster Mayonnaise

Serves 4–6 as a main course, 8 as a starter

If you serve lobster when it has just been cooked (and is barely cold) with some freshly made salads and a good homemade mayonnaise, it's absolutely magical.

2 live lobsters weighing 2 lbs (900 g) approx. each

Court bouillon
1 carrot	**bouquet garni**
1 onion	**6 peppercorns**
1 pint (600 ml/2$\frac{1}{2}$ cups) water	*no* **salt**
1 pint (600 ml/2$\frac{1}{2}$ cups) dry white wine	

Tomato salad (see below)	**homemade mayonnaise (see**
Cucumber salad (see below)	**below)**
Piped potato salad (see below)	

Garnish
tiny spring onions	**watercress**
lettuce	**segments of lemon**

Cook the lobsters following the method above and allow them to cool.

Meanwhile make the salads and mayonnaise.

Mayonnaise

I know it's very tempting to reach for the jar of 'well-known brand', but most people don't seem to be aware that mayonnaise can be made, even with a hand whisk, in under five minutes; and if you use a food processor the technique is still the same but it's made in just a couple of minutes. The great secret is to have all your ingredients at room temperature and to drip the oil very slowly into the egg yolks at the beginning. The quality of your mayonnaise will depend totally on the quality of your egg yolks, oil and vinegar and it's perfectly possible to make a bland mayonnaise if you use poor quality ingredients.

2 egg yolks, free-range
¼ teasp. salt
pinch of English mustard *or*
  ¼ teasp. French mustard
1 tablesp. (15 ml) white wine
  vinegar

8 fl ozs (250 ml/1 cup) oil
(sunflower, arachide *or* olive
oil, *or* a mixture)

Put the egg yolks into a bowl with the salt, mustard and 1 dessert-spoon of wine vinegar (keep the whites to make meringues). Put the oil into a measure. Take a whisk in one hand and the oil in the other and drip the oil on to the egg yolks, drop by drop, whisking at the same time. Within a minute you will notice that the mixture is beginning to thicken. When this happens you can add the oil a little faster, but don't get too cheeky or it will suddenly curdle because the egg yolks can only absorb the oil at a certain pace. When all the oil has been added, whisk in the remaining vinegar. Taste and add a little more seasoning if necessary.

If the mayonnaise curdles it will suddenly become quite thin, and, if left sitting, the oil will start to float to the top of the sauce. If this happens you can quite easily rectify the situation by putting another egg yolk or 1–2 tablespoons of boiling water into a clean bowl, then whisk in the curdled mayonnaise, a half teaspoon at a time until it emulsifies again.

Cucumber Salad

Serves 6

1 medium cucumber
salt, freshly ground pepper and
  sugar

1–2 dessertsp. (2–4 American
  teasp.) white wine vinegar
1 teasp. finely chopped fennel
  (herb)

Finely slice the cucumber (leave peel on if you like it). Sprinkle with wine vinegar and season with salt, freshly ground pepper and a good pinch of sugar. Stir in the snipped fennel and taste.

Tomato Salad

Serves 6

6 very ripe tomatoes
2–3 teasp. chopped fresh basil *or*
    mint

salt, freshly ground pepper and
    sugar
French dressing (see below)

Slice each tomato into 3 or 4 rounds or into quarters. Arrange in a single layer on a flat plate. Sprinkle with salt, sugar and several grinds of black pepper. Toss immediately in *just enough* French dressing to coat the tomatoes and sprinkle with chopped mint or basil. Taste for seasoning. Tomatoes must be dressed as soon as they are cut to seal in their flavour.

French Dressing

2 fl ozs (50 ml/$\frac{1}{4}$ cup) wine
    vinegar
6 fl ozs (150 ml/$\frac{3}{4}$ cup) olive oil *or*
    a mixture of olive and other
    oils, e.g. sunflower and
    arachide
1 level teasp. ($\frac{1}{2}$ American teasp.)
    mustard (Dijon *or* English)

1 large clove garlic
1 small spring onion (scallion)
sprig of parsley
1 level teasp. ($\frac{1}{2}$ American teasp.)
    salt
few grinds of pepper

Put all the ingredients into a blender and run at medium speed for 1 minute approx., or mix oil and vinegar in a bowl, add mustard, salt, freshly ground pepper and mashed garlic. Chop the parsley, spring onion and watercress finely and add in. Whisk before serving.

Piped Potato Salad

1 lb (450 g) mashed *or* Duchesse
    potato (see page 27)
2 tablesp. (2 American tablesp.
    + 2 teasp.) French dressing
    (see above)
2 tablesp. (2 American tablesp.
    + 2 teasp.) mayonnaise (see
    page 64)

2 tablesp. (2 American tablesp.
    + 2 teasp.) finely chopped
    parsley
2 tablesp. (2 American tablesp.
    + 2 teasp.) finely chopped
    chives
salt and freshly ground pepper

Add French dressing, mayonnaise, finely chopped parsley and chives to the stiff Duchesse potato. It should be of piping consistency. Taste and correct seasoning. Pipe on to individual leaves of lettuce or use to garnish a starter salad or hors d'oeuvre.

To assemble the lobster mayonnaise: Take the lobster when it is just cold (it's at its sweetest and juiciest then), split it from head to tail, remove the 'sac' which is just in the top of the head and crack the large claws.

Arrange half a lobster on each plate with some lettuce, pipe some potato salad on to the lettuce and put a little tomato and cucumber salad on the plate also. Garnish with tiny spring onions and watercress and a segment of lemon. Mayonnaise can be served separately or put into a little bowl on each plate. Serve immediately. Provide a lobster pick for each person if possible, and a finger bowl.

*Ballymaloe Hot Buttered Lobster

Serves 4 as a main course

One of the most exquisite ways to eat fresh lobster, but for perfection the lobster must come straight from the sea.

4 lbs (1.8 kg) live lobster

Court bouillon
1 carrot
1 onion
1 pint (600 ml/2½ cups) water

1 pint (600 ml/2½ cups) dry white wine
bouquet garni

4 ozs (110 g/1 stick) butter

squeeze of lemon juice

Garnish
lemon segments

sprigs of watercress, flat parsley
or **fennel**

Cook the lobsters following the method on page 63, steaming them until they are just beginning to change colour and are speckled with red.

As soon as they are cool enough to handle split them in half, as in the previous recipe, and extract all the meat from the body, tail and large and small claws. Scrape out all the soft, greenish tomalley (liver) from the part of the shell nearest the head and put it with the firmer meat into a warm bowl wrapped in a tea towel.

Heat the lobster shells. Cut the meat into chunks, melt half the butter and when it is foaming toss the meat and tomalley in it until the meat is cooked through and the juices turn pink.

Spoon the meat into the hot shells. Put the remaining butter into the pan, heat and scrape up any bits. Add a squeeze of lemon juice. Pour the buttery juices into small heated ramekins and serve beside the lobster on hot plates. Garnish with sprigs of watercress, flat parsley or fennel, and lemon segments. Hot buttered lobster should be eaten immediately.

Lobster Vol au Vent

Serves 4 as a main course, 8 as a starter

This delicious lobster vol au vent is often served on the Sunday night buffet in Ballymaloe. The filling can also be served back in the lobster shells, in which case we call it Lobster with Cream and Fresh Herbs.

12 ozs (340 g/2$\frac{1}{4}$ cups) cooked lobster meat (see previous recipe)

1$\frac{1}{4}$ lbs (560 g) homemade puff pastry (see below)

Egg wash
1 egg
1 tablesp. (1 American tablesp. + 1 teasp.) milk

2 ozs (55 g/$\frac{1}{2}$ stick) butter
$\frac{1}{2}$ lb (225 g/4 cups) sliced button mushrooms
salt and freshly ground pepper
a little freshly squeezed lemon juice
4 teasp. shallot, finely chopped
2 fl ozs (50 ml/$\frac{1}{4}$ cup) dry white wine
8 fl ozs (225 ml/1 cup) lobster court bouillon (see page 64)

roux (see glossary)
8–12 fl ozs (225–350 ml/1–1$\frac{1}{2}$ cups) cream
1 teasp. thyme leaves
2 teasp. parsley, chopped
1–2 tablesp. (1$\frac{1}{2}$–2$\frac{1}{2}$ American tablesp.) Hollandaise sauce (see page 55, omitting cucumber)

Garnish
sprigs of watercress and fennel

First make the vol au vent. Roll out the puff pastry to 5 mm ($\frac{1}{4}$ inch) thick. Use a 9 inch (23 cm) dinner plate as a guide and cut the pastry at a slight angle all round the dinner plate. Turn the pastry upside down (miraculously it will now rise in the oven with lovely straight sides). Brush carefully with egg wash and if possible refrigerate for 5 or 10 minutes. Mark the centre with a 7$\frac{1}{2}$–8 inch (19–20.5 cm) ring (we use a

Crab Mayonnaise

Crab Pâté

Ivan Allen's Dressed Crab

Clockwise from front: Warm Ray Wing with Coriander, Poached Ray Wing with Cucumber Hollandaise, Skate with Black Butter

Squid Provençal

saucepan lid as a template) and then cut half way down into the pastry with the tip of a sharp knife. Score the edges and the centre round decoratively with the back of a knife — the centre round will lift out later and act as a lid.

Place the vol au vent on a heavy baking sheet which has been sprinkled with a few drops of cold water. If possible refrigerate for 15–30 minutes and then bake in a very hot oven, 250°C/475°F/regulo 9, for 30–40 minutes approx. Turn down the heat to 220°C/425°F/regulo 7 after about 15–20 minutes and down to 180°C/350°F/regulo 4 later if it looks as though it's getting too brown. When risen and well cooked, remove the lid and scrape out the soft pastry from the inside. Return to the oven to dry the centre for a few minutes.

Meanwhile make the filling. Melt the butter in a wide sauté pan and toss the mushrooms on a high heat for a minute or two. Season and add a little lemon juice. Set aside. Add a little more butter to the pan and toss the lobster meat and green juices in the foaming butter until the meat is cooked through and juices turn pink.

Remove and add to the mushrooms, then cook the shallots gently in the sauté pan. After approx. 2 minutes add the white wine and reduce by half. Now add the lobster cooking water and reduce again. Whisk in some roux, add the mushrooms and lobster meat and blend in the cream. Boil up the sauce again for the last time, stir in the herbs and Hollandaise, taste and correct seasoning.

Reheat the vol au vent in the oven if necessary, then fill with the lobster mixture. Cover with the pastry lid. Serve immediately on a hot plate with a good green salad. Garnish with sprigs of watercress and fennel.

Note: One can of course make individual vol au vents instead of one large one. This filling will keep perfectly in the fridge for a day or two or even freezes well.

Puff Pastry

Makes 2 lbs 10 ozs (1.8 kg) approx. — enough for three 9 inch (23 cm) vol au vents *or* 28 individual $4\frac{1}{2}$ inch (11 cm) vol au vents

Homemade puff pastry takes a little time to make but it is more than worth the effort for the wonderful flavour which bears no relation to the commercial equivalent. It's essential to use butter.

1 lb (450 g/generous 3 cups)
  chilled flour (baker's flour if
  possible)
pinch of salt
squeeze of lemon juice (optional)

10–12 fl ozs (300–350 ml/
  $1\frac{1}{4}$–$1\frac{1}{2}$ cups) cold water
1 lb (450 g/4 sticks) butter, firm
  but pliable

Sieve the flour and salt into a bowl and mix to a firm dough with water and a squeeze of lemon juice. This dough is called the détrempe. Cover with greaseproof paper or clingfilm and rest for 30 minutes in the refrigerator.

Roll the détrempe into a rectangle about $\frac{1}{2}$ inch (1 cm) thick, 18 inches (45.5 cm) long and $6\frac{1}{2}$ inches (16 cm) wide (this is approximate so don't get into a fuss if it's not exactly that measurement). If the butter is very hard beat it (still in the wrapper) with a rolling pin until pliable but not sticky. Unwrap the butter and shape into a slab roughly about $\frac{3}{4}$ inch (2 cm) thick, place in the centre of the dough and fold the dough over the edges of the butter to make a neat parcel. Make sure your marble slab or pastry bench is well floured, then flatten the dough with a rolling pin, and continue to roll out into a rectangle. Fold neatly into three with the sides as accurately aligned as possible. Seal the edges with a rolling pin.

Give the dough a one-quarter turn (90°): it should now be on your pastry bench as though it was a book with the open ends facing north/south. Roll out again, fold in three and seal the edges with the rolling pin. Cover with clingfilm or greaseproof paper and rest in the fridge for 30 minutes. The pastry has now had two rolls or 'turns'. Repeat the rolling process another 2 times giving the dough 6 turns altogether with a 30 minute rest in the fridge between every two turns.

Chill for at least 30 minutes before using.

Note: Each time you start to roll the pastry place it on the worktop with the open ends north/south as if it were a book. In hot weather it may be necessary to chill the pastry slightly longer between rollings.

Prawns and Shrimps

Available all year but best in winter

It grieves me that the only way a great many people ever taste prawns is smothered in a phoney pink sauce. Prawn cocktail made with fat juicy prawns and homemade mayonnaise can, of course, be exquisite, but it is rare — and besides, there are so many other ways of treating these little luxuries with the reverence they deserve.

The other very good reason for cooking prawns carefully is that they are ferociously expensive: the price per pound may not seem so bad at first, but you must remember that what you end up with on your plate will be just one sixth of the original weight. Still, I feel that really good fresh prawns are worth every penny, so it's important to be able to recognise the best. Be totally ruthless and leave the duds for someone else!

If they are still alive, which they may be, you need have no worries about their freshness. Otherwise, make sure they smell fresh, with no trace of ammonia, that they aren't at all mushy or green around the head, and that they are still pale rosy pink.

Of course, many people don't have access to good fresh prawns — and as far as I can work out, the only prawns worth having are those that are caught and landed on the same day. In that case frozen prawns are the only option. These *can* be good, but beware of the suspiciously cheap ones that look large and smooth. They may have been dipped in water and frozen several times over to add to their bulk, in which case you will feel bitterly disappointed after you defrost them.

The **Dublin Bay prawn** is a pale pink crustacean which looks like a mini-lobster.

Shrimps

Many prawn recipes can be used very successfully for shrimps. Choosing these presents less of a problem because they are sold either alive or cooked. The ones sold in Ireland are normally pale grey when alive and bright orangey-pink when cooked. Choose the largest you can.

The **shrimp** is usually smaller than a prawn but has no large front claws. The tail curls around underneath the head.

71

How to Cook Prawns

2 lbs (900 g) whole prawns
(yields 6 ozs/170 g approx.
prawn tails)

4 pints (2.3 L/10 cups) water
2 tablesp. (2 American tablesp.
+ 2 teasp.) salt

Bring the water to the boil and add the salt. Remove the heads of the prawns and discard or use for making fish stock. With the underside of the prawn uppermost, tug the little fan-shaped tail at either side and carefully draw out the trail. (The trail is the intestine, so it is very important to remove it before cooking regardless of whether the prawns are to be shelled or not.)

Put the prawns into the boiling salted water and as soon as the water returns to the boil, test a prawn to see if it is cooked. It should be firm and white, not opaque or mushy. If cooked, remove prawns immediately. Very large ones may take $\frac{1}{2}$ to 1 minute more. Allow to cool in a single layer and then remove the shells.

Note: Do not cook too many prawns together, otherwise they may overcook before the water even comes back to the boil.

Salad of Prawns and Courgettes

Serves 4 as a starter

This salad devised by my brother Rory O'Connell both looks and tastes stunning. The courgette (zucchini) flowers are of course edible!

4 small courgettes (zucchini)
with flowers (choose shiny,
firm courgettes)
24 freshly cooked and shelled
prawns (for method see above)
a little Extra Virgin olive oil

sea salt and freshly ground
pepper
2 tablesp. (2 American tablesp.
+ 2 teasp.) homemade
mayonnaise (page 64)

Garnish
chervil *or* fennel sprigs

courgette petals

Separate the flowers from the courgettes. Remove the stamens and the little thorns from the base of the flowers.

Plunge the courgettes into boiling salted water and poach until barely tender (about 4 minutes). Remove from the pot and allow to cool slightly: they will continue to cook. While still warm cut them into $\frac{1}{4}$ inch (5 mm) slices at an angle. Season immediately with sea salt and freshly ground pepper, sprinkle with olive oil and toss gently.

To assemble the salad, arrange 6 courgette slices on each plate and place a prawn on top of each courgette slice. Cut the long courgette flowers in two horizontally and brush them with a little oil from the courgettes. Put the base section of one flower, which is an edible container, in the centre of each plate and fill with $\frac{1}{2}$ tablespoon of mayonnaise, using a piping bag if possible. Garnish the plates with the courgette petals and sprigs of chervil or fennel. Serve immediately.

Note: Mussels or shrimps may be used instead of prawns: allow 6–12 mussels or 12 shrimps per starter portion. If using lobster, allow 2 ozs (55 g) cooked lobster per portion.

Prawn Kebabs with Coriander

Serves 4–6, makes 10 kebabs approx. depending on size of prawns

$\frac{1}{2}$ lb (225 g) fresh raw prawns
(weighed after peeling)
1 small clove garlic, finely
chopped
1 shallot, finely chopped
1 tablesp. (1 American tablesp.
+ 1 teasp.) light soy sauce
2 teasp. soft brown sugar

2 teasp. ground coriander
2 teasp. freshly squeezed lemon
juice
1 teasp. fresh coriander
(optional)
1 tablesp. (1 American tablesp.
+ 1 teasp.) sunflower *or*
arachide oil for grilling

To serve
10–12 bamboo satay sticks *or*
skewers

Soak the satay sticks in water for $\frac{1}{2}$ hour before using.

Marinate the prawns with all the other ingredients (except the oil) for at least 1 hour. Thread the prawns on to the satay sticks. Just before cooking brush each kebab with a little oil. Cook over a charcoal barbecue or under a hot grill for 5–6 minutes or until just done, turning frequently. Serve hot.

Crabs

Best May—end of August

To many people, the prospect of cooking crabs is quite terrifying. Cooking them alive is a painful experience for even the most hardened cook. Besides, every time I extract the meat from a crab I keep thinking that you would really need to love the flavour already, because it's such a mucky business. To compound the difficulties, some people are actually afraid they may poison themselves with the dreaded Dead Man's Fingers. Not a bit of it! These are just the lungs and are easy to recognise. To my knowledge they aren't poisonous but have an unpleasant, chewy texture, so it's just as well to take them out.

Crabs are well worth the effort because they are still exceedingly good value in comparison to lobsters and prawns. Those you cook at home are likely to taste sweeter and more delicious than ready-cooked crabs, and an unexpected bonus is that the cooked meat freezes perfectly.

I am always surprised to discover that many people are only used to eating the white meat in the claws and are not even aware that the lovely, creamy brown meat in the body is edible. This disturbs me, because it could encourage the inhumane practice whereby unscrupulous fishermen pull the claws off crabs which are then thrown back into the water with little chance of survival. Besides, it's a dreadful waste.

The **edible or common crab** is familiar to most people, even if they haven't eaten it. It has a rigid shell, usually about 6 inches wide, two large pincers and eight small ones.

How to Cook Crab

Put the crab in to a saucepan, cover with cold or barely lukewarm water (use 6 ozs/170 g salt to every 4 pints/2.3 L water). This sounds like an incredible amount of salt but try it: the crab will taste deliciously sweet. Cover, bring to the boil and then simmer from there on, allowing 15 minutes for first lb (450 g), 10 minutes for the second and third (I've never come across a crab bigger than that!). We usually pour off two-thirds of the water half way through cooking, cover and steam the crab for the remainder of the time. As soon as it is cooked remove it from the saucepan and allow to get cold.

First remove the large claws. Hold the crab with the underside uppermost and lever out the centre portion—I do this by catching the little lip of the projecting centre shell against the edge of the table and pressing down firmly. The Dead Man's Fingers (lungs) usually come out with this central piece, but check in case some are left in the body and if so remove them.

Press your thumb down over the light shell just behind the eyes so that the shell cracks slightly, and then the sac which is underneath can be removed easily. Everything else inside the body of the crab is edible. The soft meat varies in colour from cream to coffee to dark tan, and towards the end of the season it can contain quite a bit of bright orange coral which is stronger in flavour. Scoop it all out and put it into a bowl. There will also be one or two teaspoonsful of soft meat in the centre portion—add that to the bowl also. Scrub the shell and keep it aside if you need it for dressed crab.

Crack the large claws with a hammer or weight and extract every little bit of white meat from them, and from the small claws also, using a lobster pick, skewer or even the handle of a teaspoon.

Mix the brown and white meat together or use separately, depending on the recipe.

*Ivan Allen's Dressed Crab

Serves 5–6 as a main course

When I first came to Ballymaloe my father-in-law always prepared the dressed crab for dinner. This is his recipe and very delicious it is too.

15 ozs (425 g/3 cups) crab meat, brown and white mixed (2 or 3 crabs should yield this—see above for cooking method; keep shells intact for later)

3–3$\frac{1}{3}$ ozs (85–100 g/1$\frac{1}{2}$-1$\frac{3}{4}$ cups) soft white breadcrumbs

2 teasp. white wine vinegar

2 tablesp. (2 American tablesp. + 2 teasp.) ripe tomato chutney or Ballymaloe Tomato Relish

1 oz (30 g/$\frac{1}{4}$ stick) butter
generous pinch of dry mustard or 1 level teasp. French mustard
salt and freshly ground pepper
6 fl ozs (175 ml/$\frac{3}{4}$ cup) Béchamel sauce (see below)

Topping
4 ozs (110 g/1 cup) buttered crumbs (see page 25)

Scrub the crab shells, mix all the ingredients except the buttered crumbs together, taste carefully and correct the seasoning. Fill into the shells and sprinkle the tops with the buttered crumbs (see page 25).*

Bake in a moderate oven, 180°C/350°F/regulo 4, until heated through and brown on top (15–20 minutes approx.). Flash under the grill if necessary to crisp the crumbs.

Note: 1 lb (450 g) cooked crab in the shell yields 6–8 ozs (170–225 g) approx. crab meat depending on the time of the year.

*May be prepared ahead to this point and refrigerated for 1–2 days or frozen.

Béchamel Sauce

Béchamel sauce is the rather grand French name for what many people call white sauce. It's what we call a mother sauce in culinary jargon—in other words it can be converted into many other sauces by adding extra ingredients at the end, e.g. if you add grated cheese it changes its name to Mornay sauce.

$\frac{1}{2}$ pint (300 ml/1$\frac{1}{4}$ cups) milk
a few slices of carrot
a few slices of onion
a small sprig of thyme
a small sprig of parsley

3 peppercorns
1$\frac{1}{2}$ ozs (45 g/scant $\frac{1}{3}$ cup) roux (see glossary)
salt and freshly ground pepper

This is a marvellously quick way of making Béchamel sauce if you already have roux made. Put the cold milk into a saucepan with the carrot, onion, peppercorns, thyme and parsley. Bring to the boil, simmer for 4–5 minutes, remove from the heat and leave to infuse for ten minutes. Strain out the vegetables, bring the milk back to the boil and thicken with roux to a light coating consistency. Season with salt and freshly ground pepper, taste and correct the seasoning if necessary.

Crab Cakes

Serves 5–15 depending on how they are to be served

$\frac{1}{2}$ quantity Ivan Allen's Dressed Crab (see above—no need for the buttered crumbs)
1 oz (30 g/scant $\frac{1}{4}$ cup) seasoned flour
1 beaten egg mixed with a few tablesp. milk

1–2 ozs (30–55 g/$\frac{1}{2}$–1 cup) white breadcrumbs
olive *or* sunflower oil for deep frying
Cucumber Hollandaise (optional—see page 55)

Form the dressed crab mixture into small fish cakes or little barrel shapes. Coat them in seasoned flour, egg mixture and crumbs. Deep fry until crisp and golden in hot oil, 180°C/350°F. Drain on kitchen paper. Serve with a light Cucumber Hollandaise (see page 55) or in a Fritto Misto de Mare (see page 98).

*Crab Pâté with Cucumber and Dill Salad

Serves 8–10 as a starter

This pâté which is made in a flash once you have the crab meat to hand can be served in lots of different ways. We make it into a cylinder and roll it in chopped parsley for extra posh!

5 ozs (140 g/1 cup) mixed brown
and white cooked crab meat
(for method, see page 74)
4 ozs (110 g/1 stick) softened
butter
1–2 teasp. parsley, finely
chopped

1 medium clove garlic, crushed
few grinds of black pepper
fresh lemon juice to taste
tomato chutney *or* Ballymaloe
Tomato Relish (optional)

Coating
3 tablesp. (4 American tablesp.)
parsley, finely chopped

To serve
Cucumber salad (see page 65)

Garnish
flat parsley, fennel *or* chervil
fennel *or* chive flowers, if
available

Mix all ingredients (except the parsley for coating) together in a bowl or, better still, whizz them in a food processor. Taste carefully and continue to season until you are happy with the flavour: it may need a little more lemon juice or crushed garlic. Form the pâté into a cylinder, roll up in greaseproof paper, twist the ends like a Christmas cracker and chill until almost firm.

Spread one-quarter sheet of greaseproof paper out on the work top, sprinkle the chopped parsley over the paper, unwrap the pâté and roll it in the parsley so that the surface is evenly coated. Wrap it up again and refrigerate until needed.

Make the cucumber salad.

To serve, arrange a circle of cucumber slices on individual white plates and put one or more slices of pâté (depending on the size of the roll) in the centre of each. Garnish with flat parsley, fennel or chervil and fennel or chive flowers if available. Serve with crusty white bread or hot toast.

*Tomatoes Stuffed with Crab Mayonnaise

Serves 6 as a starter

Crab mayonnaise is very versatile. It is delicious used as a filling for cucumber or tomato ring as well as a stuffing for tomatoes. It also marries very well with a simple tomato salad (see page 66) or as a first course for a dinner party.

5 ozs (140 g/1 cup) mixed white and brown fresh crab meat (1 medium-sized cooked crab should yield enough—for cooking method, see page 74)
6 very ripe firm tomatoes
salt and freshly ground pepper

6–8 fl ozs (175–225 ml/¾–1 cup) homemade mayonnaise (see page 64) *or* a couple of tablesp. French dressing (see page 66) instead of some of the mayonnaise
½ teasp. onion, finely grated

Garnish
small lettuce leaves
garden cress *or* watercress

edible flowers e.g. chives

Cut the tops off the tomatoes, remove the seeds with a melon baller or a teaspoon, season with salt and turn upside down to drain while you prepare the filling.

Mix the crab meat with the mayonnaise, grate some peeled onion on the finest part of the stainless steel grater and add ½ teasp. of the onion juice to the crab. Taste and season if necessary.

Fill the crab mixture into the tomatoes and replace the lids. Arrange a bed of lettuce and salad leaves on a white plate. Serve 1 large or 2 small tomatoes per person. Garnish with sprigs of fresh herbs and some edible flowers.

Scallops

Best October–February

I have always found scallops irresistible, not only because of their delicious sweet flavour but also because of the beautiful shell. I can never bear to throw scallop shells away: I use the deep ones as containers for many fish first courses and give my children the flat tops to make a scallop edge for their flowerbeds.

Like prawns, scallops should be bought either live or very recently dead! Once again, check for any smell of ammonia and if you notice the slightest whiff, forget them and buy something else.

Scallops are bivalves with distinctive whitish-brown or pinkish shells. The Great Scallop is the variety normally available in the shops, but look out for the smaller Queen scallops as well.

Warm Salad of Scallops with Toasted Pine Kernels and Avocado

Really fresh pine kernels are difficult to find—they go rancid very quickly, so ask to taste one before you buy. If you do find good ones, buy extra and freeze some.

Serves 4 as a starter

8 scallops
1 oz (30 g/¼ cup) pine kernels
3 tablesp. (4 American tablesp.) olive oil
1 tablesp. (1 American tablesp. + 1 teasp.) balsamic vinegar *or* white wine vinegar

½ teasp. Dijon mustard
salt and freshly ground pepper
selection of salad leaves, e.g. lamb's lettuce, radicchio, frizzy lettuce, watercress
1 ripe avocado

Garnish
a few sprigs of fresh chervil

Detach the corals from the scallops. Cut the scallop nuggets in half across the centre and dry well on kitchen paper. Toast the pine kernels under a hot grill or in a moderate oven until golden (5 minutes approx.). Whisk the olive oil, vinegar and mustard together to make a vinaigrette and season to taste. Wash the lettuces well, shake dry and tear into bite-sized pieces.

Just before serving season the scallops with salt and freshly ground pepper and fry quickly in a non-stick pan for about 1 minute on each side, turning once only. Remove from the pan and keep warm.

Cut the avocado in half. Peel, slice thinly and fan out, putting a quarter on each plate. Put the salad leaves in a deep bowl. Toss with a little of the vinaigrette and place a portion of salad on each plate in a mound beside the avocado, arrange the slices of scallop over the salad and sprinkle with chervil leaves and toasted pine kernels. Serve immediately.

Scallops Mornay

Serves 12–14 as a starter, 6–7 as a main course

12 scallops	creamy milk
dry white wine and water to cover	salt and freshly ground pepper
3 ozs (85 g/¾ cup) shallots *or* onion, chopped	2–3 ozs (55–85 g/½–¾ cup) Cheddar cheese, grated
1 oz (30 g/¼ stick) butter	1 heaped tablesp. (2 American tablesp.) parsley, chopped
5–6 ozs (140–170 g/scant 3 cups) mushrooms, chopped	Duchesse potato for piping around the shells (optional—
2 heaped tablesp. (5 American tablesp.) flour	see page 27)

Put the scallops in a medium-sized stainless steel saucepan and cover in half white wine and half water. Poach for 3–5 minutes (be careful to simmer and not to overcook). Remove the scallops and reduce the cooking liquid to 10–12 fl ozs (300-350 ml/1¼-1½ cups) approx.

Sweat the chopped shallots gently in butter until soft (about 5-6 minutes). Add the chopped mushrooms and cook for 3-4 minutes more. Stir in the flour and cook for a further 1 minute. Add creamy milk to the scallop cooking liquid to make up to 1 pint (600 ml/2½ cups) and add to the saucepan. Taste the sauce, reduce until the flavour is really good and season.

Cut the scallops into 4 and add to the sauce with some of the cheese and the parsley. Decorate the scallop shells or serving dish with Duchesse potato, fill the centre with the scallop mixture and sprinkle the top with the remaining cheese.

Just before serving, reheat in a moderate oven, 180°C/350°F/regulo 4, until just bubbling (20 minutes approx.).

Note: This mixture also makes a delicious filling for pancakes or vol au vents.

Scallops with Beurre Blanc and Chervil

Serves 4 as a main course, 8 as a starter

This is the most exquisite way to eat really fresh scallops. A non-stick pan is essential for this recipe.

12 large scallops

salt and freshly ground pepper

Beurre blanc sauce

3 tablesp. (4 American tablesp.) white wine

3 tablesp. (4 American tablesp.) white wine vinegar

1 tablesp. (1 American tablesp. + 1 teasp.) shallots, finely chopped

1 generous tablesp. ($1\frac{1}{2}$ American tablesp.) cream

6 ozs (170 g/$1\frac{1}{2}$ sticks) cold unsalted butter, cut into cubes

salt

pinch of ground white pepper

freshly squeezed lemon juice

Garnish

fresh fennel *or* **chervil sprigs**

First make the Beurre blanc. Put the wine, wine vinegar, shallots and pepper into a heavy-bottomed stainless steel saucepan and reduce down to about $\frac{1}{2}$ tablespoon. Add the cream and boil again until it thickens. Whisk in the cold butter in little pieces, keeping the sauce just warm enough to absorb the butter. Strain out the shallots, season with salt, white pepper and lemon juice and keep warm in a bowl over hot but not simmering water.

Just before serving, slice the white part of each scallop in half so that you have two round pieces of equal thickness, and keep the coral intact. Dry on kitchen paper. Just before cooking season the scallops with salt and freshly ground pepper. Heat the non-stick pan and put the scallops directly on to it in a single layer, not too close together. Allow to cook on one side until golden before turning over, then cook the other side.

Spoon a little very thin Beurre blanc on to a large hot white plate for each person (thin it if necessary by whisking in warm water), arrange the slices of scallop and coral on top of the sauce, garnish with fennel or chervil and serve immediately.

Oysters

Native Irish oysters best when there is an 'r' in the month
Imported Pacific oysters available all year round

It take a certain amount of courage to taste your first oyster. You gulp it down, try a few more . . . and before you know where you are you may find yourself addicted and all too ready to sample a dozen or two at a time. Whether the oyster's aphrodisiacal qualities have anything to do with its appeal I can't say—but sure it's worth a try anyway!

I think we are extremely fortunate in Ireland to have access to both our own native oysters—without a doubt the best in the world—and the Pacific variety. The flat Irish oyster is at its best when there is an 'r' in the month. It has such a wonderful salty tang that it seems a sacrilege to overpower it with anything as pungent as tabasco or horseradish sauce. All it needs is a few drops of lemon juice. The Pacific oyster, now very successfully cultivated in Ireland and available all year round, is also delicious *au naturel*, but its deeper shell makes it ideal for cooking too. I often find that people who can't under any circumstances be persuaded to touch an oyster raw find them surprisingly delicious when they are cooked.

Oysters must be still alive when you buy them: the shells must be tightly shut. They should be stored packed in layers, deep shell down, in as small a container as possible. Put a weight on top to prevent them from opening and use them as soon as you can.

The greatest problem for many people, particularly when they get an unexpected present of oysters, is how to get the damned things out of their shells. Pincers, screwdrivers and all sorts of tools are resorted to, but honestly it's well worth investing in an oyster knife or one of those new oyster crackers which make the job so simple. Follow the instructions for oyster opening in the Plate of Irish Shellfish recipe on page 95.

One final word of warning: don't drink whiskey with oysters. It seems to cause a chemical reaction which can make you feel extremely ill, with symptoms similar to food poisoning. A glass of Irish stout, champagne or dry white wine would be a better bet.

The **Irish or European oyster**, *Ostrea edulis*, is more rounded than the longer, deeper **Pacific** variety *Crassostrea gigas*. This one is also known as the Rock, Portuguese or simply Gigas oyster. Its shells are worth keeping to use as containers for herb butter when you serve pan-grilled fish.

*Hot Buttered Oysters

Serves 4 as a starter

These wonderfully curvaceous oyster shells tend to topple over maddeningly on the plate so that the delicious juices escape. In the restaurant we solve this problem by piping a little blob of Duchesse potato on the plate to anchor each shell.

12 Pacific (Gigas) oysters
1 oz (30 g/¼ stick) butter

½ teasp. parsley, finely chopped

To serve
4 segments of lemon
4 ovals of hot buttered toast
  (optional)

Open the oysters and detach completely from their shells (see Plate of Irish Shellfish recipe, page 95). Discard the top shell but keep the deep shell and reserve the liquid. Put the shells into a low oven to heat through. Melt half the butter in a pan until it foams. Toss the oysters in the butter until hot through—1 minute perhaps.

Put a hot oyster into each of the warm shells. Pour the reserved oyster liquid into the pan and boil up, whisking in the remaining butter and the parsley. Spoon the hot juices over the oysters and serve immediately on hot plates with a wedge of lemon.

Alternatively discard the shells and just serve the oysters on the hot buttered toast. The toast will soak up the juice—Simply Delicious!

Angels on Horseback

Serves 4 as a starter, up to 16 as a cocktail snack

Guaranteed to covert even the most determined oyster hater!

16 oysters

8 very thin streaky bacon rashers

To serve
buttered toast

Open the oysters (see Plate of Irish Shellfish recipe, page 95). Drain and reserve the juice for another recipe. Discard the shells. Cut the rind off the bacon rashers if necessary. Cut each rasher in half and wrap a piece around each oyster. Secure with a wooden cocktail stick. Cook under a preheated grill for 5–8 minutes depending on the size of the oysters, or until the rashers are crisp (turn over half way through cooking). Serve immediately on little rounds of hot buttered toast.

Mackerel with Green Gooseberry Sauce

Chargrilled Squid with Fresh Chilli Sauce

Monkfish Spedino

Prawn Kebabs with Coriander

Warm Smoked Salmon with Cucumber and Dill

Turbot with Carrot and Chives

Cockles, Clams, Palourdes and Roghans

Best when there is an 'r' in the month

I'd love everybody to discover that there is a marvellous gastronomic side to all these little shells which most people have only ever used to decorate sandcastles on the beach as children. I was delighted to see that since the Dublin millennium a few years ago, cockles and mussels alive, alive-o can be enjoyed once again in Dublin pubs—even though the unfortunate side-effect of this is higher cockle prices. But Irish coasts also have a bountiful supply of the cockle's near relations, clams, palourdes and roghans. The next time you come across them, buy them, bearing in mind that the French pay a fortune for these little Irish bivalves which can be ours for next to nothing. Remember that they should be absolutely fresh and tightly closed, and remove the little 'exhaust pipe' from each after cooking. The recipes in this section suit all four varieties.

Cockles have a small, hinged, ridged shell, almost like a tiny scallop.

Clams, also hinged, are often much larger than cockles but have a smoother shell. They come in many varieties, all of them roundish.

Palourdes (also known as carpet shells) are a variety of clam, much loved by the French, Spanish and Portuguese who often eat them raw. The shells are white, yellow or light brown with darker brown streaks.

Roghans are a type of clam with concentric ridges on the shell which develop into wart-like spines on the edges, hence their other name, Warty Venus.

Clams, Palourdes or Roghans Gratinée

Serves 6–8 as a starter

This recipe may also be used for oysters but they will take longer under the grill.

48 clams, palourdes *or* roghans
1 tablesp. (1 American tablesp.
  + 1 teasp.) olive oil
4 streaky bacon rashers (rindless)
4 ozs (110 g/1¼ cups) mushrooms,
  finely chopped
1 tablesp. (1 American tablesp.
  + 1 teasp.) parsley, chopped

salt and freshly ground pepper
2 tablesp. (2 American tablesp.
  + 2 teasp.) buttered crumbs
  (see page 25)
3 tablesp. (4 American tablesp.)
  Gruyère cheese, finely grated

Heat the olive oil in a frying pan, fry the rashers until crisp, remove and cut into tiny pieces. Toss the chopped mushrooms quickly over a high heat in the bacon fat, add the chopped parsley and season with salt and freshly ground pepper. Add the diced rashers and allow to cool. Mix the buttered crumbs with the cheese.

Put the clams in a covered pan over a low heat, remove as soon as the shells open, save the juice, remove the outer rind and the 'exhaust pipes' (siphons). Cover the clams first with the mushroom mixture and then sprinkle a little of the cheese and buttered crumb mixture on top.* Arrange in an ovenproof dish, brown under a hot grill for 3 or 4 minutes and serve immediately.

*May be prepared ahead to this point.

Steamed Cockles or Clams with Fresh Herbs

Serves 2 as a main course, 4 as a starter

This recipe is also delicious for mussels, or a mixture of cockles and mussels.

2 lbs (900 g/1 quart) cockles *or*
  clams
1 oz (30 g/¼ stick) butter
4 ozs (110 g/1 cup) onion,
  chopped
2 cloves garlic, peeled and
  crushed
½ pint (330 ml/1¼ cups) dry white
  wine

2 teasp. chopped parsley
1 teasp. chopped thyme leaves
1 teasp. chopped fennel (herb)
1 teasp. chopped chives
roux (see glossary)
4–5 fl ozs (120–150 ml/½ cup
  approx.) cream

Garnish
chopped parsley

Melt the butter in a saucepan, add the chopped onions and crushed garlic and sweat for a few minutes. Add the wine and herbs and cook for 5–6 minutes, then add the well washed cockles or clams, put the lid on the saucepan and cook for 4–5 minutes until all the clams are open.

Pour the liquid into another saucepan, bring to the boil, thicken very slightly with roux, add cream and bring to the boil again. Taste, pour over the clams and sprinkle with chopped parsley. Serve in hot deep bowls with crusty white bread.

Mussels

Available all year but best when there is an 'r' in the month

If you have seen and read *Simply Delicious 2* you will know by now that I am messianic about mussels! I feel it's high time everybody shook off any lingering inhibitions and tried cooking these succulent shellfish. They are now widely available, both farmed and wild, in Ireland, and are also incredibly cheap. The great thing about mussels is that they can be used in so many ways, either in recipes on their own or to embellish other fish dishes.

While there are indeed places around our coasts where you can safely gather mussels and other types of shellfish, for those in doubt it is probably wiser, for the small amount of money involved, to buy them. No fishmonger worth his salt will risk his reputation by selling mussels that have not been purified.

Freshness is easily checked by tapping against a worktop any shells which are not tightly shut. If they tighten, well and good; if they don't, throw them out! Never take a risk with shellfish.

The **Blue Mussel** is the main variety sold in Ireland. Everyone is familiar with its dark blue or blackish shell, which can vary in size. Buy the biggest you can: the plumper they are, the more delicious.

Mussel Salad with a Julienne of Vegetables

Serves 4 as a starter

2¼ lbs (1 kg/2¼ quarts) fresh mussels
1 small carrot cut into very fine julienne strips 2 inches (5 cm) long
¼ cucumber peeled, seeded and cut into julienne strips 2 inches (5 cm) long
1 avocado (optional)
¼ pint (150 ml/generous ½ cup) homemade mayonnaise (see page 64)

8 leaves lollo rosso *or* oakleaf lettuce *or* enough lamb's lettuce to make a ring on a plate
1–2 tablesp. (1½–2½ American tablesp. approx.) French dressing (see page 66)

Garnish
**very finely chopped chives and
chive flowers**

Check that all the mussels are tightly closed, wash under cold water and drain. Put into a wide saucepan and cover with a lid or a folded tea towel. Steam open on a medium heat (this will only take 2–3 minutes). Remove the mussels from the pan just as soon as the shells open, allow to cool, remove the beards and discard the shells. Strain the mussel liquid and reserve.

Put the julienne of carrot and cucumber into a bowl of iced water and season with sea salt. Peel and dice the avocado. Dilute the mayonnaise with the mussel cooking liquor to a light coating consistency.

To serve, arrange a circle of lettuce leaves on each of 4 white plates. Mix the avocado with the mussels. Arrange a little mound of this mixture in the centre of each plate and coat with the light mayonnaise. Drain the julienne of carrot and cucumber, toss in French dressing and season with salt and pepper if necessary. Place about 1 dessertspoon of this on top of the mussels. Sprinkle with finely chopped chives and chive flowers and serve.

Spaghetti with Mussels, Tomato and Basil

Serves 6 as a main course, 12 as a starter

Fun to make and delicious to eat. Leave a few of the mussels in their shells and add a fresh chilli if you like.

6 lbs (2.7 kg/6 quarts) mussels *or*
**a mixture of cockles, clams
and mussels**
$\frac{3}{4}$ lb (340 g) spaghetti
**4 tablesp. (5 American tablesp.
+ 1 teasp.) olive oil**
2 large cloves garlic, sliced
**6 ozs (170 g/1$\frac{1}{2}$ cups) onions,
chopped (use some spring
onion/scallions if available)**

**1 lb (450 g) very ripe tomatoes
peeled and sliced *or* 1 × 14 oz
(400 g) can tomatoes, sliced**
freshly ground pepper and sugar
**1 tablesp. (1 American tablesp.
+ 1 teasp.) chopped parsley**
**1 tablesp. (1 American tablesp.
+ 1 teasp.) torn basil**

Garnish
parsley and basil

Check that all the mussels are tightly closed and wash well. Put into a wide saucepan or frying pan, cover, put over a low heat and as soon as the shells start to open, pick them out immediately. Remove the beards, discard the shells and keep the mussels aside. Strain and save the liquid.

Heat the olive oil in a stainless steel saucepan, add the sliced garlic and cook for a few seconds, add the onion, cover the saucepan and sweat over a gentle heat until soft but not coloured. Add the peeled, sliced tomatoes and the mussel liquid. Season with freshly ground pepper and sugar. Simmer with the lid off until well reduced.

Meanwhile cook the spaghetti by putting it into plenty of boiling salted water, boil for 2 minutes, remove the pan from the heat and cover tightly. Leave the spaghetti in the water for 15 minutes.

Add the mussels to the sauce, stir in the chopped parsley and basil. Taste and correct seasoning. Strain the spaghetti, pour the sauce over it, toss, sprinkle with more parsley and basil and serve immediately in a hot pasta dish.

Gratin of Mussels and Potato

Serves 4–6 as a main course

Everyone loves this gratin recipe. It's cheap to make and very tasty — and you could do variations on the theme.

3 lbs (1.35 kg/3 quarts) mussels	1¼ lbs (560 g) cooked potatoes
8 tablesp. (10½ American tablesp.) olive oil	sea salt and freshly ground pepper
8 ozs (225 g/2 cups) onion, chopped	2 ozs (55 g/½ cup) buttered crumbs (see page 25)
10 fl ozs (300 ml/1¼ cups) dry white wine	2 large cloves garlic, peeled and crushed
1 tablesp. (1 American tablesp. + 1 teasp.) shallot or spring onion (scallion), chopped	2 tablesp. (2 American tablesp. + 2 teasp.) chopped parsley
2 sprigs of parsley	1 oz (30 g/¼ cup) finely grated Parmesan cheese
2 sprigs of thyme	

Sweat the onions in half the olive oil in a heavy bottomed saucepan until soft and golden brown (about 7–8 minutes).

Meanwhile check that all the mussels are tightly closed, wash them and put them into a stainless steel saucepan with the wine, shallot and herbs, cover and cook on a medium heat. As soon as the shells open remove to a tray to cool. Strain the mussel cooking liquor, take the mussels out of the shells, remove the beards and put the mussels into the liquid.

Slice the potatoes, toss in the remaining olive oil in a frying pan, season with sea salt and freshly ground pepper, then layer the potatoes, mussels and onions in a gratin dish and pour on some of the mussel liquor to come quarter way up the dish. Mix the buttered crumbs with the garlic, chopped parsley and cheese. Sprinkle over the top.

Bake in a moderate oven, 180°C/350°F/regulo 4, until hot and bubbly — 15–20 minutes. Flash under a grill to crisp the top if necessary. Serve with a good green salad.

Sea Urchins

Best when there is an 'r' in the month

It was about fifteen years ago that we first came across sea urchins in a roundabout sort of way. My husband had a frantic phonecall from a West Cork fisherman who was urgently in need of mushroom chips. When these were delivered to the airport it was discovered that he was starting to export sea urchins to Paris, and we were given a few baskets to try. Nobody we asked had the least idea what to do with them: even now cookbooks aren't exactly full of ideas for sea urchins! Myrtle Allen came up with an idea for sea urchins with mayonnaise and they have been a favourite on the menu at Ballymaloe ever since.

It was only while I was doing the research for this book that I uncovered the most confusing thing about these prickly little fellows. The large, pinkish ones commonly referred to as Edible Sea Urchins are not, apparently, edible at all. It is the roe of the smaller, dark purple urchins (*Paracentrotus lividus*) that we find so delicious to eat either raw or cooked.

With so many sea urchins around the west and southwest coasts of Ireland, it seems to me a great pity that more people don't try them, instead of simply putting the shells on the mantelpiece as an ornament. If you need further encouragement, look again to the Continent where all the urchins that are so enthusiastically consumed come from Ireland. Like all shellfish, they should be perfectly fresh when cooked.

The genuinely edible **sea urchin** is a ball of dark purple spikes. Urchins are usually collected by divers. You may find smaller ones in rock pools—be sure to remove them with gloves!

Sea Urchins with Homemade Mayonnaise

Serves 4 as a starter

Those prickly little sea urchins so common on the west coast of Ireland can require an act of faith to tackle for the first time. Real connoisseurs eat them raw and our French customers make all sorts of appreciative 'ooh là là' noises when they find them *au naturel* on their plates. However, I still enjoy them more when they have been cooked briefly and when the inside corals have been sieved and mixed with a little mayonnaise. We then dip little soldiers of toast into the delicate purée and eat the rest with a spoon just like a prickly egg!

4 sea urchins	**2 slices hot buttered toast**
2 tablesp. (2 American tablesp.	
+ 2 teasp.) approx. homemade	
mayonnaise (see page 64)	

Cook the sea urchins for 3 or 4 minutes in boiling salted water. Drain and allow to cool. Scrape the prickles from the top of the shell. Lever out the plug with the end of a teaspoon or the point of a kitchen scissors. Cut a larger hole. Scoop out the coral, sieve it and mix with the homemade mayonnaise. Taste. Add more mayonnaise if necessary. Fill back into the shells and serve with fingers of toast.

Sea Urchins Nature

Serves 4

4 sea urchins

Garnish
4 segments of lemon   **a few sprigs of parsley**

Scrape the prickles from the top of the shell. Lever out the plug with the end of a teaspoon or the point of a kitchen scissors. Cut a larger hole. Put each sea urchin on to a plate and serve with just a segment of lemon and perhaps a sprig of parsley for garnish.

Note: Sea urchin coral can also be added to Beurre blanc or Hollandaise sauce.

Mixed Fish Dishes

It would be a great pity to take a one-at-a-time approach to fish, because seafood lends itself to all sorts of marvellous combinations. A mixture of pink and white fish can look very pretty on the plate; fish terrines with different layers look stunning too; and several sorts of shellfish served together can be a memorable treat, with their subtly different yet complementary flavours.

If you need more persuasion to mix and match, try that crispy Italian favourite, Fritto Misto, or dazzle your friends with a tempting Mediterranean fish stew. The recipes in this section are slightly labour-intensive but well worth the extra effort for a special occasion. All are guaranteed to add panache to any dinner party and leave your guests begging for more!

A Plate of Irish Shellfish with Homemade Mayonnaise

Serves 6 as a substantial starter

The highlight of a recent trip to Paris was a *Plateau de fruits de mer* which I ate at a restaurant on the Champs Elysées. A huge variety of shellfish was served piled high on a special stand filled with crushed ice, with bowls of mayonnaise and French dressing and segments of lemon underneath. Bliss! When I complimented the waiter a happy hour later and inquired about the origin of the shellfish, he told me that most had come from the southwest coast of Ireland, so there you are now!

All or most of these:

6 sea urchins	**18 cockles**
18 Dublin Bay prawns *or* **24**	**18 roghans**
shrimps	**12 palourdes**
18 mussels	**6 native Irish oysters**

Accompaniment
**homemade mayonnaise
(see page 64)**

Garnish

6 segments of lemon	**seaweed (optional)**
sprigs of wild watercress *or*	**a few periwinkles (see page 96)**
fennel	**and maybe a whelk**

Cook the sea urchins in boiling salted water (1 tablesp./1 American tablesp. + 1 teasp. salt to 2 pints/1.1 L/5 cups water) for 4–5 minutes, remove and allow to get cold.

Cook the prawns following the instructions on page 72. Allow to cool and then remove the shells.

If the shrimps are live, cook them in boiling salted water also for 2–3 minutes or until the shells have changed colour from grey to bright orangey-pink. If there is any trace of black on the heads cook them for a little longer. Drain and allow to cool in a single layer.

Wash the mussels, palourdes, roghans and cockles and check that all the shells are tightly closed. They can then all be opened in the same manner as follows. Spread the shells in a single layer in a heavy bottomed saucepan. Cover with a folded tea towel or a lid and put the pan on a low heat for a few minutes. Remove the shellfish as soon as they open (if any refuse to open, discard them). Keep the liquid which will exude from the shellfish as they open: it's wonderful for fish soup or a sauce or for thinning mayonnaise to be served with shellfish.

Remove the beards from the mussels and discard one shell and loosen the mussel from the remaining shell so that the guests won't have to tussle with their fork. Remove the outer rind and 'exhaust pipes' (siphons) from the palourdes and roghans and discard one shell. Nothing needs to be removed from the cockles except one shell also.

When the sea urchins are cold, scrape the prickles off the top with a spoon or brush, then tap the centre with the bowl of a teaspoon; the shell usually cracks like an egg so the centre can be lifted out. Be careful not to lose any of the precious juices and make sure to remove any splinters of shell from the centre. It will be necessary to provide a teaspoon for eating the sea urchins and a fingerbowl should also be provided if the guests are to peel the shrimps or prawns themselves.

Not long before serving, open the oysters. You will need an oyster knife for this operation. Place the oyster on the worktop, deep shell down. Cover your hand with a folded tea-towel and hold the oyster firmly. Put the tip of the oyster knife into the crevice at the hinge of the oyster, push hard and then quickly twist the knife. You need to exert quite a bit of pressure, hence it is essential that the hand holding the oyster is protected, in case the knife slips. When you feel the oyster is opening, change the angle of the knife and, keeping the blade close to the shell, slice the oyster off the top shell in one movement. Then run the knife underneath the oyster in the deep shell and flip it over: be careful not to lose any of the delicious juices.

Now arrange the shellfish on large white plates. Place a tiny bowl of homemade mayonnaise in the centre. Garnish with a segment of lemon and a few spigs of fennel, wild watercress or flat parsley or blanched seaweed.

To blanch seaweed, e.g. bladderwrack, for garnish, plunge sprigs into boiling water for a few seconds, remove immediately and refresh in a bowl of iced water. It will turn bright green. This can be fun to do but it should be used fairly soon because it begins to get slimy quite quickly. It's edible but not very palatable!

*Periwinkles with Homemade Mayonnaise

As a child I well remember sitting on the pier at Lahinch, and screwing up my face and thinking and probably saying 'yuk' as my father heartily enjoyed eating periwinkles out of a newspaper cornet. Years later I picked up the courage to taste them and discovered that they are indeed delicious.

fresh live periwinkles
boiling salted water (6 ozs/170 g
   salt to every 4 pints/2.3 L/10
   cups water)

homemade mayonnaise (see page
   64) *or* garlic mayonnaise (see
   page 12)

Bring the water to the boil, add the salt and the periwinkles, bring the water back to the boil, strain off the water and allow the periwinkles to get cold. Serve with mayonnaise or garlic mayonnaise. Some people like to dip them in vinegar. Either way you will need to supply a large pin for each person to extract the winkles from the shells. A few winkles would be very good served on the plate of shellfish also.

Ballymaloe Fish Terrine with Tomato Coulis

Serves 10–12 as a starter

Most fish terrines are based on sole, and though they are delicious when served hot, they can be very dull and bland when cold. This layered fish pâté is a great favourite. Its content varies depending on the fish available to us.

First layer
4 ozs (110 g) cooked shelled,
  shrimps *or* 6 ozs (170 g)
  prawns (cut up if large, so that
  they will cover the base of the
  tin)
$\frac{1}{2}$ clove garlic
$3\frac{1}{2}$ ozs (85 g/scant 1 stick)
  clarified butter (see page 15)

1 teasp. thyme leaves
2 teasp. lemon juice
1 tablesp. (1 American tablesp.
  + 1 teasp.) parsley, finely
  chopped

5 × 8 inch (13 × 20 cm) bread tin

Prepare the tin by lining it neatly with a double thickness of clingfilm. Crush the garlic into a paste with a little salt. Melt the butter in a saucepan with the thyme leaves and garlic and then bring to the boil. Add the shrimps or prawns and simmer gently for 3–5 minutes. Add lemon juice to taste. Allow to cool, pour into the tin in an even layer, sprinkle with a little chopped parsley and chill while you prepare the next layer.

Second layer
4 ozs (110 g) smoked mackerel *or*
  smoked herring flesh, free of
  bones and skin
3 ozs (85 g/$\frac{3}{4}$ stick) softened
  butter

lemon juice to taste
1 tablesp. (1 American tablesp.
  + 1 teasp.) parsley *or* chives,
  finely chopped

Blend the smoked mackerel and butter together in a food processor. Taste and add lemon juice if necessary. When shrimps have set hard spread this paste on top of them in an even layer. Sprinkle with a little more parsley or chopped chives. Refrigerate while you prepare the next layer.

Third layer
4 ozs (110 g) cooked salmon, free
  of skin or bone
lemon juice to taste
3 ozs (85 g/$\frac{3}{4}$ stick) softened
  butter
1 small clove garlic
pinch of salt

$\frac{1}{2}$ teasp. fennel, finely chopped
  (optional)
salt and freshly ground pepper
1 tablesp. (1 American tablesp.
  + 1 teasp.) parsley, chopped

Crush the garlic into a paste with the pinch of salt. Blend it with salmon and other ingredients in the food processor. Taste and correct seasoning. Smooth the mixture over the first two layers and sprinkle with a layer of parsley and keep chilled.

Fourth layer

5 ozs (140 g/1 cup) mixed brown
  and white crab meat, cooked
4 ozs (110 g/1 stick) softened
  butter
2 teasp. parsley, finely chopped

1 medium clove garlic, crushed
black pepper
2 teasp. tomato chutney *or*
  Ballymaloe Tomato Relish

Blend all the ingredients together in a food processor. Spread this final layer on to the fish terrine. Cover with clingfilm and press down well to compact the layers and chill until needed.

Tomato Coulis

1 lb (450 g) tomatoes, as ripe as
  possible
$\frac{1}{2}$ oz (15 g/$\frac{1}{8}$ cup) onion, chopped
2 teasp. white wine vinegar
2 tablesp. (2 American tablesp.
  + 2 teasp.) olive oil

1 level teasp. salt
1 level teasp. sugar
black pepper
2 basil leaves *or* 4 fresh mint
  leaves

Skin the tomatoes (see page 78 for method), halve and take out the pips. Blend the tomato flesh with the other ingredients and sieve if necessary. Taste and correct seasoning.

To serve the terrine, turn out on to a chilled dish and remove the clingfilm. For a buffet, decorate with salad leaves and with any fresh herbs and herb flowers you can find. Serve in slices and offer a little tomato coulis with each helping. Alternatively, pour a little tomato coulis on to individual white plates, place a slice of the fish terrine on top and garnish with tiny sprigs of fennel or cress.

Fritto Misto de Mare

Fritto Misto literally means 'mixed fry' and certainly sounds much better in Italian than in English. Fritto Misto de Mare is a mixture of fish which is either pan fried or deep fried, served with an appropriate sauce or sauces. It is delicious only if you use a variety of very fresh fish and good olive oil to fry in. Please, please don't use the atrociously poor quality oil on general sale for deep frying. It will ruin the flavour of even superb fish and the smell will permeate your hair and clothes and, if you don't shut the doors, your whole house as well!

A typical Fritto Misto de Mare might include:

deepfried prawns, dipped in
batter (see page 12)

deepfried mussels, dipped in
batter (see page 12) *or* flour,
egg and crumbs

deepfried monkfish collops
dipped in batter (see page 12)
or flour, egg and crumbs

deepfried fillets of plaice *or* sole
dipped in batter (see page 12)
or flour, egg and crumbs

deepfried crab cakes (see page
76)

a slice of salmon pan-fried and
served with Maître d'hôtel
butter (see page 30)

squid with garlic butter (see
page 28) *or* dipped in batter
and deepfried

Sauces
Tartare sauce (see page 46)
Orly sauce (see page 13)

Garlic mayonnaise (see page 12)

Garnish
sprigs of parsley *or* watercress

segments of lemon

Put a selection of cooked fish on hot plates, garnish with parsley and
lemon and serve with the selection of sauces. Some deepfried vegetables are also delicious with the Fritto and help to spin out the fish.

Italian Fish Stew

Serves 8 as a main course

This fish stew looks very sophisticated with the mussel shells and
squid peeping through. Use it as a basic formula for whatever firm fish
and shellfish you can get spanking fresh.

$1\frac{1}{2}$ lbs (675 g) monkfish, ling,
hake *or* haddock, cut in 2 inch
(5 cm) pieces

1 lb (450 g) squid, cut in $\frac{1}{4}$ inch
(5 mm) rings *or* strips (use
tentacles also)

2 lbs (900 g/2 quarts) mussels,
washed

4 tablesp. (5 American tablesp.
+ 1 teasp.) olive oil

$\frac{1}{2}$ lb (225 g) streaky bacon,
rindless, cut into $\frac{1}{2}$ inch (1 cm)
cubes

2 cloves garlic, peeled and
crushed

1 onion, sliced

2 red peppers, seeded, quartered
and thinly sliced

2 green peppers, seeded,
quartered and thinly sliced

1 chilli, seeded and chopped
(optional)

6 large very ripe tomatoes,
peeled and sliced

salt, freshly ground pepper and
sugar

7–8 leaves fresh basil

Garnish
parsley, freshly chopped   **basil leaves**

Heat the olive oil in a saucepan or casserole, add the bacon and fry until crisp and golden. Add the garlic and onion. Cover and continue to sweat for 5–6 minutes, add the peppers and chilli if using, cover and sweat for a further 5–6 minutes.

Scald the tomatoes in boiling water for 10 seconds, pour off the water immediately and peel. Slice and add to the casserole, season with salt, freshly ground pepper and sugar and continue to cook until the vegetables are soft (25–30 minutes approx.).*

Just before serving add the torn basil leaves and white fish to the simmering casserole. Cook gently for 3–4 minutes or until the fish turns white and is almost cooked. Then add the squid and mussels, cover and cook gently for 2–3 minutes or until the mussels open. Taste, correct seasoning, pour into a hot pottery dish and serve scattered with freshly chopped parsley and basil leaves. Remove mussel shells if you like (but we like to leave them in).

*May be prepared ahead to this point.

Note: Spaghetti may be served with this stew $-\frac{1}{2}$–1 lb (225–450 g) depending on how much pasta you like to eat.